Tales From Planet Gumption

MICHAEL STOCKDALE

Michael Stockdale

Sale of this book without a front cover may be un-authorized. If this book is coverless, it may have been reported to the publisher as "unsold or destroyed" and neither the author nor the publisher may have received payment for it.

Tales from Planet Gumption is a work of fiction. Names, characters, places, and incidents are the products of the author's imagination or are used fictitiously. Any resemblance to actual events, locales, or persons, living or dead, is entirely coincidental.

Copyright © 2012 Michael Stockdale

All rights reserved

Cover illustration © Michael Stockdale

ISBN-13: 9781481219631

ISBN-10: 1481219634

Tales from Planet Gumption

DEDICATION
Our four vibrant children, good friends and Byron Bay

Michael Stockdale

Acknowledgement
Maureen
Always

Tales from Planet Gumption

Contents

Acknowledgements.............................P4

Jack London Never Died......................P6

The Hairdresser's Daughter....................P57

Via Qantas......................................P103

Putsi..P160

Michael Stockdale

Jack London Never Died

Heavy rain swept down along the Strand, past the Junction Hotel out and beyond the Cradle Bridge. Beneath its iron frame soft mouthed mullet ruled and multiplied. Further upstream, dour mothballed Navy vessels swayed and lurched against the tide. Westward-ho, the Irish Sea showed off its muscles and danced a jig with the Cumbrian coastline. Any second now, the mournful wail from the town's Pied Piper its Shipyard hooter. All embracing and guaranteed to awaken the dead. Howled, "Get a move on," to succored workers, relaxed behind locked iron gates. Pleased to be safe. Knew it was seven thirty.

This daily ritual of shifts on the move never changed the route of Gumption's weary Council bus. Not very long ago, packed with noisy smoking swearing smelly men weighed down by ex-Army overcoats and hobnailed boots. Pulled up outside 123 Lord Street empty; groaned, spluttered nearly died. In the attic, four flights up the local 'wanderer' stirred his loins. Wide awake, watched and studied an agile spider stroll behind his faded curtains. Tried and tested by the aroma of bacon and eggs that emanated from downstairs. Idle thoughts, some vocalized.

"No hot bath for you my bonny lad. What? No fucking hot water?"

Words he said to himself. No swearing or liquor allowed in the house. No one went to church or read the Bible out aloud. Yet on pay days Dad donated at the Pub in exchange for Jehovah's and Salvation Army periodicals later used for kindling.

Tales from Planet Gumption

"Dad's disconnected the HW immersion heater."

Up in arms with the town's National Grid. Flew the Union Jack; spent a fortune on postage stamps threw baskets of paper at bureaucrats. Had forgotten the 'wanderer' was about to leave for distant shores. Christ Almighty! It was far too late for the bonny lad to visit Gumption's Public Baths. Pay eighteen pence for the favor; free soap shampoo extra.

The 'wanderer's nose shaped like the prow of an ocean liner; suited the occasion. Skinny body dressed in boxer shorts; stoically pumped fifty press-ups. Shivered, dashed down two flights of stairs to the bathroom. No fucking soap! Salvaged one tiny piece of carbolic and washed to the waist in freezing cold water. Pulled on his jeans and trusted ex-Army and Navy Stores string vest. Soon he would leave this house with no soap or hot water, migrate and set sail from Liverpool to Canada. Mam yells up stairs.

"Yah breakfast is ready."

Spotted a note pinned to his bedroom door from his comedian brother.

"Go easy with the soap. Please send money. Keep your legs crossed, all the best, Joe."

The parlor fire roared its approval when he entered. The latest news; Dad may ration coal. His Mam beamed like a lighthouse cried.

Michael Stockdale

"Here it is then bonny lad," gingerly lowered a full large dinner plate. Bacon and eggs; fried bread, tomato some thick slices of black pudding and brand new bottle of HP sauce. In five seconds flat, his favorite mug full of strong black tea, umpteen slices of toast and a jar of home-made marmalade. She who fussed paused stood to one side. Her hair uncombed the poor old thing, still wore yesterday's pinafore.

The rain had stopped and behind the house on 'The Backs' parked on Her Majesty's Theatre cinder car-park sat a young woman inside her father's Funeral Hearse. Two inch long finger nails painted black. Dressed in mourning, black hat and veil. Yelled at him from the driver's seat 'to mind out for the fake silver candlesticks with his trunk,' normally occupied by coffins. Struck a grand condescending pose, very stylish; patted her immaculate beehive hairdo turned up her nose cringed at his luggage.

"*That* thing must be older than the Mayflower! Where did you find *that*? If someone left it in the street nobody would pinch it."

The trunk supplied by another close pal ubiquitously known as the Pie Lady. Its paper thin, ancient profile strapped with rope and stout leather straps gratis. Eased expenditure and saved him brass.

"Now then our Douglas, I hope you're not superstitious but we'll have none of those Royal waves to anyone in Dalton Road. Be serious, no whistling. My Dad would have a fit. The things *I've* done for you."

Douglas V for Victor Warrington grinned and nodded. Brown eyed

Tales from Planet Gumption

with black curly hair, the picture of innocence an added plus. Vociferous ex-car salesman, high seas mariner resplendent in his recycled brown tweed suit, size ten incompatible country brogues. Windsor knotted tie, bland buttoned down ivory colored shirt, appreciated the lift and the fact that the redhead down below wore black fish-net tights. Her official black dress dry cleaned by Courtesy Cleaners suspended from a coat hanger. Cooed and giggled, tempted providence.

"Don't get frisky this is just for you and old times. Don't forget to write."

"Smashing, you look great. I owe you one. Look, I've no idea if I'll even like Canada never mind be gone for good. I'll write and be back in no time you'll see."

Dressed in black she had qualified in beautifying dead bodies. The idea of being left on the shelf did not occur to her. She was after all eligible. Her Dad's business flat out prospered in overworked Gumption.

June 1961. Doug the washed to his waist erstwhile lover man had long past failed to ignite and complete his Night School engineering education. Settled for padded voluptuous brassieres; feminine breasts, the bigger the better flouted by the town's assertive teen-aged shop assistants. Born and bred in the northwest UK seaboard town of Gumption named after an Aristocrat's champion whippet. Seeded by failed romantics, WW2 casualties and bombed out buildings. But, in the sixties thrived by heck; three nights a week overtime, three week-ends out of four that equated to untold wealth. Up for grabs for anyone,

Michael Stockdale

particularly tradesmen employed in the local Shipyard

So be it, his Night School Lecturer accurately assessed Douglas zero visionary. That little bugger Warrington always chose the simplest route. Jogged, leisurely through apprenticeship majored average with chicks and heavily in motor bikes. Filed his official indentures in the same drawer as his underpants, his only other 'trophy' hung framed on his bedroom wall. Kipling's poem IF, donated by and cleaned once a week by his old Mam.

Doug's dalliance with the ladies not yet set in stone. His sine curve matched the profile of his nose registered work as life threatening scatterbrained and as to be expected fell foul with authority. Aged 21 he had quit the trade to sell used-cars for Mac's at Ambleside and made a handsome packet. Called up, "Your Country Needs You," ill-advised by non-too bright relatives and instead signed up with Fischer Tankers and joined the Merchant Navy. Sailed the seven seas for washers; tipped his hat to Joseph Conrad and was nearly swept overboard. Recovered and moved up a notch with career defining Cunard Steamships with a bone to pick with distant relative God.

The sudden unexpected recent sobering death of the so very young adroit Germaine, someone he courted long as a teenager and talked of Canada. Her short life and death unnerved him. She was affectionately respected and indirectly one of the reasons he was bound for Canada.

Doug's mentor his down to earth Rigger by trade swarthy rational Dad held the fort glued to library books. Was not ambitious, prejudiced or color blind, accepted Doug's snap decision bookmarked his page and generously contributed five pounds credit. To be returned in the hand if not used, or repaid on another day. His wiser younger brother Joe worked as Mechanic at Low Brow's Garage and thought the idea of Canada a joke. She who pressed sheets part-time at Gumption's Lakeland Laundry his fat old Mam, baked countless rock cakes to celebrate his departure; her standard knee jerk reaction to all perceived calamities. Yet when he reached down and gently kissed farewell to his battle-axe tough old Church Street boarding house Grandmother, she showed considerable emotion. A seldom seen rare tear rolled down her powdered cheek, her jaw sagged. Her damp cigarette remained unlit.

Doug's trunk drew a crowd that showed respect, doffed their caps at Gumption's Railway Station when unloaded from the town's established Funeral Director's Hearse. Half-dressed Agnes went savage on the Hearse's horn. The man who sold tickets gave Doug a hand, almost died from laughing. Tickled pink Doug stood and waited on miserable Platform Two close to hysteria with the sendoff.

Sobered up the moment he climbed on board faceless Brit Rail and finally arrived in wind swept Liverpool. His trunk commandeered and assigned to Edmonton, Alberta Canada. For the very first time he embarked in civvies and not in uniform. His host one of Canadian Pacific's liners now on 'movements' appeared crammed with hundreds of optimistic migrants and perhaps some of Britain's finest youth.

It took just two days out of Liverpool for him to shed the novelty as passenger. Watched it fade into obscurity, disenchanted by a few hard faced bogey-eyed females' lackadaisical shipboard brevity. Bored to death with the ship's resident two bob four-piece Band, one swayed back ageing singer called Vince the bogey-eyed females' obvious target. Two more days to go; apprehension with a capital 'A' set in amongst the single men. To the man, frantically exchanged ideas or contacts and modified their plans daily. Doug's embarrassing ethos he kept to himself. Played the odds and did not possess a genuine job offer. Hard faced relied on an introductory, "Jobs for everyone" standard circular from Alberta's Government Boiler Department.

Doug had few tangible paper qualifications when compared with nearly everyone on board. All he possessed was an indentured apprenticeship Fitter and Turner's certificate from Pickersgill's Shipyard, his Mercantile Marine Discharge Book with detailed log and two personal references. One hastily scribbled by Gumption's Doctor Noonan Flanagan written as if in Latin or disguised as an influenza prescription. The other grand and eloquent written on parchment paper by his kind old school Headmaster with a very bold hand but totally bias. Summed up Doug had very little to bullshit about.

The idea of going to Canada had fermented as far back as when Doug was eighteen, hidden under a four inch gun mounting in the Shipyard's Gun Shop. Two or three apprentices, him included speculated where they would like to go when they finished their 'time.' Canada always came up trumps. Doug's weakness then and for most of his life were chicks. His latest foray, deep thinker flighty Germaine the trainee school teacher. Germaine's mother worked at the same laundry as his Mam and both approved. But their romance attracted too many lovers' tiffs. One moment she would be all over him and next she would send him packing. She had this arty thing about the sea and Walney Island's sandy foreshore. Hot summer's days passed locked together bollock naked, hidden by Lawrence of Arabia's dunes chased away by hungry horse flies. This horny girlfriend of his carried two secrets. One shared solely with her parents. The other held at bay; Teachers' College Principal, passionate prim, Mr. Harold Stitt.

Doug day dreamed while others strutted on deck and recalled last Christmas when Germaine's card arrived on board the RMS Queen Mary out the blue. Attached her London address and telephone number, brief note, 'Call in in whenever in town,' the usual kisses. Someone in Gumption must have let on about his never dreamt of prestigious naval role, Marine Engineer on one of the most famous Liners in the world. Lauded, each time she berthed at New York's Pier 92. Outran German U-Boats during WW2 and carried 'the boys' back home to America.

Six weeks duty at sea meant two weeks furlough, maybe drop in to see Germaine before travelling north. Booked into a London B&B near Euston Station determined to track her down. Found her flat padlocked when he arrived. Rummaged about and finally caught up with the building's cleaner who was suspicious, awkward and reluctant to tell him anything. Too many questions then opened up.

"She's dead luv, died suddenly last week, sorry luv," and walked away.

Doug leant on the Canadian liner's handrail and recalled his disgust at the time. It made so much sense then and no sense at all now. On their very last tenuous date she had talked of Canada and said she would go, yet later that day he had packed her in for good. Childish thoughts filled his head. Back from leave. Miserable, not much chat so much so the lads on the 'Mary caught a whiff of personal drama and sympathized.

News traveled fast and on Cunard's elegant old lady it was no different. His Liverpool based Superintendent's ear close to the deck knew all about it when he called in Liver Buildings. He had overseen Doug's progress through an entire rank and was sour about the outcome. The Superintendent still wore his faded russet tweed jacket, elbows worn out patched with thin red leather. One still flapped in the wind until he finally nodded.

"Please take a chair Douglas. I believe the entire ships' crew is aware of your sad loss. This resignation of yours is on one hand understandable and on the other hand stupid and impulsive. With more time spent at sea you could sit for your ticket."

"If I come back can I rejoin the Queen Mary?" pleaded Doug weakly.

At this point he waited for an answer and got the one he did not want. His plea hit hollow ground. The seasoned Superintendent then explained the reason why, with compromise.

"That would create precedence and that's the last thing we'd want to happen. However, under the circumstances and your excellent record let's say three months compassionate leave at your own expense and leave it at that. One thing, why Canada, we have ships which go there all the time?"

Bound for Montreal, Canadian Pacific's liner plowed along leisurely and on time. It's mainly migrant passengers' overconfident males; University men who had worked in the City in Finance or Marketing. The women on the other hand could not care less. Partied until dawn and blamed the silvery moon for all their indiscretions. The only organized professional migrant Doug met and befriended was Kurt a short, smartly attired German pastry cook. He had secured a real job in Banff. Produced a photograph of what appeared to be a large Bavarian castle, its battlements covered with snow surrounded by rugged mountains. Immensely satisfied with the new opportunity vanished shacked up with a fine young German widow.

But for out of kilter Doug his reality check was defused by a cheerful young blonde landed English girl and travelling companion an older brunette who knitted. His dialect intrigued them. Conversely, his limited vocabulary amused them and suggested he was harmless. They generally met daily at Morning tea out on deck. Their daily chat arena and sat together on deck-chairs. It was she who knitted, plain Jane flat chested who raised her head and asked the question.

"Tell me Douglas, where is Gumption? Speaks of Yorkshire or North East Coast? I've never heard of it."

Click, click continued knitting, shook her head from side to side. Her with white teeth full of lead tittered; lightened up queried.

Michael Stockdale

"Up north you say? You're going to Canada for pecuniary ah monetary reasons? Yet you haven't got a job to go to?"

Here we go again, thought the optimist. Pecuniary, monetary two more words he did not know the meaning of. It was at moments like this he felt like an alien when the 'crack' became heavy, kept simple with a joke.

"There's nothing pecuniary about me lass, I'm as normal as any bugger. And as for monetary, I'd never live the life of one of those Monks. It'd send me batty."

These cracks often saved the day. They roared with laughter and opened up more about themselves. The knitter was a paid companion for the delicate pretty girl, travelling as far as Vancouver to an off shore island with the daft name of Rupert to stay with relatives. The pretty girl said her brother was the Adjutant at Britain's top Military College. Neither of these references struck any bells. His gamble to edge a little closer she evaded. Would smile, nearly tempted excuse herself then vanish. Both had ridden horses in Epping Forest and attended Palace parties. Asides that fell on hollow ground. Both had lousy legs and as an expert he viewed both as pleasant company but nothing to write home about.

Four days had passed. Sheer panic sped throughout the ship as if Cholera, spent packing and unpacking bags. Frustration expressed by the City men grouped in neat three-piece pinstriped business suits. Those with military experience pursued modes of attack but more suited for

Tales from Planet Gumption

English High Streets than Canada's prairies. By comparison Doug's simple plan was to find the cheapest place to stay in Montreal then catch a train to Edmonton.

Doug was not really alone, most were solely there on a promise, no job to go to. No wads of cash in their shoes. The word on deck pointed to Montreal's YMCA; the cheapest joint in town. Up front as Doug secured his berth it seemed half the ship's company had joined him. Signed on then nowhere to go, stood around in solemn uncomfortable groups. Overdressed, starched collars, worsted tweed exposed to high temperatures and turned in early. Close to midnight. Heavy handed optimistic knocks; armed muscle Montreal Cops there to check for women they might find bedded. Gave up and left with a parting shot.

"You won't find a fucking virgin over fourteen between Montreal and Vancouver," greeted by jeers and two pairs of shoes.

Doug's stay at Montreal's YMCA was a seedy affair. Its gritty foyer extended to the street; more long queues as he left and eventually rolled up at Montreal's Railway Station. His Pie Lady's trunk already consigned to special goods to be picked up and signed off in Edmonton. Free of baggage he climbed aboard his first bluff powerful Canadian Pacific train. Impressed by its air-conditioned interior and his own comfortable adjustable seat he would eat and sleep in over the next four days. English twang a twang voices, laughter; the sight and sound of Kensington's plain Jane knitter stitch one pearl and her toothy goofy companion personally escorted by the train's Conductor.

Michael Stockdale

Doug cried out, "Hi-yah," his words lost by the tall Conductor's deep baritone voice; pressed strides and attendant balls sang out.

"This is the wrong carriage, ladies. First Class: two carriages up. Move along there please."

Washed to his waist but with real soap and hot water Lord Street's pride and joy's self-imposed one meal a day journey expected to take four days. The adjustable seat his 24 hour bed and easy chair. Grub from the snack bar or by silver service, with flowers if in First Class Dining Car. His funds limited. Dictated one main meal per day, Spaghetti and Meat Balls, kept up appearances; wolfed down but only after Kensington digested and departed. This inane façade he scrapped almost immediately. Dozed in style, left the women to it and adapted. Absorbed and excited by the harsh wild desolation viewed from his carriage window. The outside imagery surprisingly softened by occasional long stops in small western towns.

Here, few would alight and walk the elevated crude outstretched covered boardwalks. Undaunted, Doug strode the counterpane, heard his footsteps echo. Walked amongst real western memorabilia, smelled the earth; passed locked unpainted shacks, littered with sleeping deadbeats and passing cowboys. The latter, lounged in slow talking spread-eagled gangs. Stained battered straw Stetsons faded blue jeans. Hand rolled aromatic cigarettes. Shadowed, by huge pyramids of stacked pumpkins; miniscule shop windows thick with dust. Terminated by rugged Ford 4WD trucks parked haphazard sharp against the skyline.

Tales from Planet Gumption

As the train headed further west women's dresses grew longer. Pop music submitted to Blue Grass and blared from some hidden transistor radio. Each woman escorted by stern unsmiling older men dressed in long old fashioned clothes. Grizzled, tough skinned, slit eyed clad in tight stove pipe trousers. Stared unblinking beneath stiff rabbit skin sombreros and smoked or chewed unlit black cheroots. Rapt by the theatre Doug watched on fascinated. No one would believe him back home. This had to be the very Last Train to Yuma, Doug's favorite western seen three times at Gumption's Palace Cinema.

Then abruptly and in the middle of a vast plain they passed what might have been a coal mine. Its perimeter dominated by semi-circular high banks of debris or workings, as if prehistoric giant footsteps in no particular order. Perched on each bank, clusters of small patch-worked home-made cottages; scant washing on the line. It seemed like the end of the world where gangs of grubby pale faced children ran alongside the train tracks and waved. Doug waved back but was not impressed. Thought it was shithouse. Felt like throwing cash and threw all he could afford one measly $10.00 note. He may have been the only person on the train to throw money. Jesus Christ, he had never seen such abject poverty in his entire life. The last thing he expected to witness in booming Canada.

Four dawns, introduced Doug to four different people. One an inarticulate full blooded Red Indian brave spent all his time in the carriage toilet. Its door left wide open, one hand pulled the chain several times. The brave intrigued; did not have a clue where the water came from. Shook his head, walked away then returned five minutes later and repeated the whole process once again.

Another was a grizzled old French Canadian who wore an ill-fitting red tartan jacket, ochre colored trousers and purple cowboy boots growled.

"Bon jour Monsieur, you travel far? Do you like cock-books? I have plenty."

Placed his battered bag down next to his seat and threw several lurid magazines on their shared table Doug could never buy in Gumption's Market. He ignored and fell asleep straight away.

His next visitor was a serial drunk who carried a quart bottle of whiskey in his inside pocket, kindly offered at ten minute intervals morning to dusk. The last but by no ways least was a prim, disheveled middle aged woman, dressed in a severe dark blue two piece. Her face almost hidden by large horn rimmed glasses, one rim heavily taped, arrived and sat opposite, was blunt.

"My name is Bella, I'm bound for Calgary. What's yah name honey? Yah look English. Where yah bound?" She too found his dialect quaint, and inside an hour appeared to take a fancy to him.

But she did not leave Calgary's station instead kept him company and waited for the incoming Edmonton train. He had no idea how old she was, but she was long gone as a teenager and on the nose. The Edmonton train arrived on schedule and she climbed aboard breathed heavily and sat next to him. At first Doug had been flattered but she looked as old as his mother and he did not have the courage to dump her. She followed him when he got off at Edmonton and linked his arm like ole' friends. His first concern was to pick up the Pie Lady's trunk, his worldly goods and all he possessed. They joined a queue and the man with the mandatory eye shade accepted his paperwork. Veered left, then returned to tell him some very bad news and suggested he should inspect the damage. On the deck lay his Pie Lady's trunk smashed in little pieces. His companion suddenly lost interest and silently slipped away as he hesitated; signed off paperwork, accepted the offer of several old hessian sacks and carefully stuffed them with his life's belongings.

Meanwhile, on another platform Bella stealthily approached what she perceived as another target and jammed her left knee firmly into his crotch. It stopped him dead, her face two inches away as he attempted to slip sideways.

"That'll cost yah fifty bucks big fellah," she grated in his ear, "One more fucking move I'll call security."

Trapped, unable to move surrounded by witnesses he passed over what notes he had. She then broke away slowly, backed off. Turned on heel and scurried off in the opposite direction. It took her only two or three minutes and never failed to work. Soon she would do the very same thing again but in a busy street. Within an hour, cash in her pocket she was on another train to Calgary.

By the time Doug came to his senses and glanced around his female limpet had disappeared. She had seen his miserable possessions. Relieved she had gone he grabbed his bulging hessian sacks and hailed a taxi, minutes later panicked when it braked outside a huge modern high rise building.

"What's this pal?" cried an incredulous Doug.

Gob-smacked, by the space age shimmering granite and towering tinted windows. Its entrance partially blocked by an unending line of limousines. The driver laughed and insisted that this was his final destination. Smiled, pointed to the bold neon sign above which confirmed it was indeed Edmonton's YMCA. And as his Auntie Alice might have said, 'Now then *that* was a nice surprise.'

Doug's room was vast by English standards, ultra-modern and luxurious compared to his parents' now banned hot water bath at 123 Lord Street, until further notice by his authoritarian Dad. Surprisingly, the YMCA had its own restaurant, full size swimming pool and a multitude of other facilities. Based on his immediate needs, he had enough cash to stay there for at least two weeks, provided he kept to one meal a day. So there he was, well done Sunshine, scrubbed up inside his own personal shower. One hundred degrees Fahrenheit outside, him inside an air conditioned kitted out room, equipped for 'away from home' students was close to Palace life.

Six hours later, his snooze disrupted by the wails of countless Police car sirens and erratic gun fire cowboy style outside his window. Intermittent loud guttural shouts, screams of pain then plain silence;

memories of Johnny Cash's 'Don't take your guns to town,' first heard anchored in Rotterdam and long before he joined Cunard.

Dawn, found Doug in one of Edmonton's stalagmite Alleys; on either side high rise glazed pillars built from steel and concrete. Huge faceless buildings so many windows where few open doors embraced Alberta's mid-western air, not much folk about no obvious movement. When, suddenly instant bedlam his body absorbed by a surging massive rolling crowd of mainly men, each one physically ejected onto the pavement. Defeated, sprawled and scattered. Sheer panic expressed in their crazed eyes. Some stopped dead exactly where they stood or fell. Flopped on pavements; countless feet inside roadside gutters as if glued unable to move. Watched intently by six Police cars, parked directly opposite. Hardened, unsympathetic grim faced men monitored the blood and bone canopy as it enveloped the street and sidewalks.

Doug restricted and entangled with the destitute, attempted to find out what was going on, but found few could or would speak English. Except for a man in rags who touched him for a dollar. He told Gumption's full blown optimist this was a daily routine adopted by Doss Houses in the street, all or most were unemployed or homeless migrants and blamed the God damned recession. Yet another new descriptive word Doug did not know and asked him to explain.

"The next best thing to a depression, no work, mass sackings, on the streets," then lost interest and walked away to touch someone else for another dollar.

Michael Stockdale

Doug was substantially subdued by the time he entered Alberta's Migration Office. Lined up, to be interviewed by short and sheepish Hiram; an outwardly reclusive young man of similar age who checked his file and commandeered his passport. Hiram expressed condolences on the death of his trunk, wrote down an address where he would find McCloud's Boiler Department.

It did not take long for Doug to find his office, second floor inside another faceless building two blocks away. Six or eight weeks had passed since he had received McCloud's badly interpreted letter, or about the same time he had received his acceptance missive. It did not really matter because McCloud never expected to see the applicant in the flesh. He had just sent their standard letter and made up numbers counted bodies he had since forgotten.

Silver haired, mystified McCloud shook Doug's hand like a long lost brother but seemed unsure of his ground. He recalled the name but was unable to source his file. His feathers ruffled by the young man's attitude.

"This is the Boiler Department isn't it?" queried Doug.

And brandished McCloud's heaven sent heavy gauge paper. Growled,

"This is *your* letter pal?"

Disconcerted by the cantankerous kid the much older Albertan played for time and humored him, sat Doug down with a mug of instant coffee.

Tales from Planet Gumption

Whistled a tune as he weighed up his visitor through rimless glasses as Doug too weighed up McCloud Gumption style.

McCloud's appearance was silver service, tamed cropped head. Fitted white short sleeved shirt stretched at the waist which oozed managerial confidence. Impeccable grey slacks, hand stitched brown leather belt prominent Buffalo Head buckle, solid copper attached, offset by ornate high heeled polished boots. McCloud read aloud from copious notes with apparently no luck said glibly sotto voice.

"Let's have a look at your qualifications son and I'll tell you how you score."

Doug's list of double-spaced 'qualifications', took up just two lines. McCloud lifted his head and looked Doug squarely in the eyes.

"What's this, no UK National Certificate or City and Guilds or High School certificates?" Spluttered, "How the fuck did you get in? Guys like you are expected to have English qualifications comparable to ours and to my mind there's fuck all here."

Produced a spotless handkerchief blew his nose, cleared his throat, observed by Doug 'as fuck off now before I thump you.'

Fergus McCloud meant a piece of paper which said certificate or diploma. The only certificate Doug possessed was his Shipyard indentured apprenticeship and to his eyes was all they needed to know. It had not occurred to him to include details of his Mercantile Discharge book. He had it handy, pushed self-consciously across McCloud's spacious desk.

Ex-ocean going ticketed mariner McCloud was now on familiar ground. He had one similar back at the ranch and recognized it as legal tender. This UK Ministry of Transport Mercantile Marine Discharge Book identified Warrington as a registered Marine Engineer. Second mate McCloud read Doug's Discharge Book slowly from cover to cover at least twice. Relaxed and pleasantly surprised to find it contained evidence he had sailed with Fischer's Tankers, his last appointment on the 'God damn Cunard's Queen Mary,' rated excellent in Doug's Discharge Book! McCloud roared with laughter howled at the moon.

"Fucking hell, you left the best God damned fleet to come to Canada? Why? We can't match that."

Spluttered, coughed went almost purple, excused himself and left the room. More loud hysterical laughter outside the open door as McCloud vocalized the interview to inner sanctum cronies.

"I've got me a dumbass critter that left the fucking Queen Mary to find work here. Beat that, out here in mid-west Canada!"

McCloud's gratuitous jeers sliced through the paper thin walls like a knife with the result Doug became twice as resolute. The man he was dealing with was a patronizing bastard with considerable power. Edmonton was littered with migrant casualties and it was not a laughing matter. Mentally Doug decided not to leave this office until his position

Tales from Planet Gumption

was clarified.

It was a subdued McCloud perhaps chastened by a superior, who compromised and rated Doug at the very bottom of Alberta's accreditation list. His certificate would read Third Class Alberta Steam Plant Engineer. McCloud smugly added.

"There are no Albertan positions available for this classification."

Then printed out the thought to be worthless certificate, with a damning hand-written note at the bottom, 'This classification is subject to further qualifications,' attached his signature. Brusquely shook the loser's hand, showed him the door. Short of clouting him Doug left. Dramatically cut adrift from Gumption's Black Horse Hotel, Fischer Tankers and now Cunard, but still his own man stumbled into the street black as thunder. There was no job and for one brief moment he felt cheated. When in reality he now had something really tangible, a piece of local currency. Something he did not have twenty-four hours earlier.

During the following week Doug applied for many strange two bob jobs all or most paid washers, some already taken or withdrawn. Fortunately most interviews were with sincere, sympathetic helpful people. Two or three already partially affected themselves would persist and write down names and contact numbers of obscure outfits who may be hiring. One hundred degrees in the sun was one favorable substitute for the endless rain back home albeit serviced by only one meal a day. In many ways he sensed he had been reduced to begging and it was inevitable he would revert back to his long list of mining companies.

Michael Stockdale

They seemed the only tangible form of employment alternatives even though he had no desire to work at any mine. Stood twice in one particular street outside two major Canadian Mining Houses but lacked courage and chickened out.

Now in his second week, Doug the itinerant migrant compiled and sent off cramped yet overly confident aerogrammes to his parents and dear Agnes. Wrote and lied, said he was doing fine. Opened an account with the Royal Bank of Canada with one dollar, and on the same afternoon bit the bullet; took pot luck entered Keno Hill Mine's City office and talked to one of its grave, but distantly interested Personnel.

It was not what Doug would have called an interview, more like a chat about his background and willingness to travel. They took leisurely copies of his brand new abridged Alberta Steam Engineer's Certificate and trade certificate. Then asked him to fill in a quantity of forms and to finally relax and wait in the foyer. It seemed as though he had been there for ages when the very first person he had spoken to wandered in. Sat down in an opposing chair and gave him some surprising news.

"A replacement Steam Plant Engineer is urgently required in Elsa at Keno Hill Mine Power Station immediately. I faxed them your details and the job is yours to think about and to let me know your decision by lunch tomorrow."

The interviewer was used to stunned silences. Patted Doug's shoulder like he was a retriever dog added.

Tales from Planet Gumption

"We'll hear from you tomorrow then?"

Negative thoughts sped through Doug's head as fast as if he had missed the last train from anywhere on a Saturday night. Let them know by tomorrow? Holy shit, he was desperate almost broke. He hardly slept that night. He had never read Jack London's 'Call of the Wild.' He did not care that Keno Hill was in the Yukon. Next day and stiffened by the knowledge his YMCA deal would be dead in twenty-four hours he fronted Personnel's desk the moment they opened. He was expected. His name printed on a brand new Manila folder front and center at reception. He signed his employment acceptance slip with haste and listened intently to further instructions.

"Take this taxi voucher and flight tickets. Be at the Airport early tomorrow morning as directed, have a good trip, welcome aboard."

On the same day he walked into a one man Barber shop and told him to shave his head. His curly black locks covered the floor as he confided his story to hysterical hairy Tony the sympathetic Italian Barber. Tony spoke in broken English like a machine gun fresh out of bullets. Thought Doug had done very well and was very lucky to find a job, and no, he had never heard of Keno Hill. The following morning Doug joined an outgoing YMCA queue to pay his account, as another parallel queue formed of incoming clients. Startled; recognized a now haggard, scruffy bunch from his Liverpool ship and baled them up.

"Hey, what's happening lads? I thought you were all fixed up in Montreal?"

Michael Stockdale

The last thing Doug expected was an agitated tirade from long haired twang a twang Lord Wilfred.

"Christ! You've no idea old chap, what we've been through. We paid a jolly fortune for this immaculate late model 4WD in Montreal but it conked out after just two hours on the road. We traded for a Campervan and truth to tell failed to find work on our entire journey here. Sadly old chum, our financial situation is grim, very grim indeed."

Doug empathized but chose not to rub salt in Wilfred's wounds or to disclose his luck instead gave him and his disenchanted fellow travelers his stash of addresses, phone numbers plus contact names. Said so-long, knew the drum, shook hands and cleared off.

Cash wise he had five dollars in his pocket when he arrived at the Airport. Here he joined a very short queue headed by two hairy German miners recruited by Keno on the same flight, who like him travelled light. One, had the build of a Jockey, the face of a smiling ferret introduced himself as Karl. By stark comparison his sidekick Heinrich, the width of a barn, looked like an all-in wrestler just grunted. Both spoke English badly, and Doug certainly did not speak German but as time passed the unlikely trio hit it off. Their itinerary was to fly to the Yukon to a the city of Whitehorse, stay overnight then by light plane fly to Mayo, then overland by vehicle to Elsa, c/o Keno Hill Mines.

Whitehorse turned out bleak but prosperous and active. One drink before bunking down seemed a good idea but Doug's new pals had no

Tales from Planet Gumption

cash. So he shouted them both with his last five bucks and magnanimously told the barman to keep the change. Pre-dawn the thud from the butt of a souvenir black Luger on their cabin door. Owned by Big Jim Mac Vies: Half Cherokee and half of Glasgow: Face to face, very ugly, impossible to see past. Called them punks, chewed an unlit cigar, grumbled profusely but was pleased they travelled light.

Ordered the punks to climb on the tray of his battered utility and sit at the rear. Pressed on the gas and took off at great speed into the Territory's hinterland. Pulled up minutes later outside an ill lit primitive airstrip then guided them to his small single engine 4-seater aircraft. One by one they climbed aboard, secured all doors and fastened seat belts.

Big Jim, their unlikely pilot crouched impassively silent up front his long plaited hair down to his shoulders; folds of fat around his middle that made him look nine months pregnant. Took his time and fired up the heavily loaded tiny craft. The plane seemed to prance as if short of breath like a hesitant dancer. Bounced erratically along the uneven surface then lifted off almost immediately. Curled upwards and turned north.

There appeared to be nothing visible down below to the ex-Mariner man, except darkened unanimated territory. Doug gulped inwardly, defined it bastard shit, insecure uncompromising and hostile. Yet sooner than later somehow he felt more relaxed and more curious than apprehensive now his adventure had really started. Then gravity, sensed as the craft pointed earthbound. Clouted mother earth bounced several times before landing formally; taxied. There were no farewells. No one uttered a single word. Their overland transport, a giant truck parked next to the only one roomed, no electricity black shacked latrine block for miles. Already to go, the three shook hands with Mac Duff the truck's driver and climbed aboard his monster Chevrolet.

Two immaculate automatic rifles were strapped across Mac Duff's rear window. One heavy gauge S&W holstered revolver attached to its dash. Inside one of Mac Duff's fur lined boots, the polished bone handle of a Bowie knife protruded ominously. Both hands tattooed in large Gothic print with the words, Love and Death. His distorted hooked nose appeared to be broken several times. Almost toothless, except for one long raw yellow fang exposed outside his narrow slit mouth used to open cans of American beer. Quietly spoken with a lisp he confided he had married a squaw who was the daughter of the Chief. Extremely proud he had fathered ten children and all his kids had perfect teeth. Lived on the Indian Reserve and was the blood brother of the Indian who drove Keno Hill's biggest Caterpillar front end loader.

By now Doug was convinced that an overloaded light single engine plane over rough terrain was a dodgy means of transport meant for desperate people. But their journey inside a Chevrolet crossbred truck come military tank would be far worse. They pressed north beneath an unchanged miserable carpeted sky through a smudged, indistinct grey land ahead, unsure if it was day or night. By now there was now little or no conversation, just grunts and farts with the occasional stop for a piss. All second class passengers unwashed and unfed, had accepted their fate content to sleep. Until outside the terrain dramatically changed and their long based vehicle's arthritic suspension bottomed on each rise then bottomed again at its base. Heinrich awoke and was violently sick. Karl then needed a shit, but the driver who did not speak German but understood panic, stopped by the first convenient ditch.

Maybe they drove alongside the Yukon River; it's fast moving impatient waters chopped seemed overly anxious. Through and out of the burnt out remains of one or two large eerie forests but saw very little wild life. No wolves, grizzly bears, elk nothing four legged except when they approached Keno Hill. When suddenly, alongside eight yelping Husky dogs on a parallel dry track abused by their crazed driver. Lost control caught up in the reins of his ram-shackled sled, dragged along bodily and in shreds suddenly gone. An incident ignored by a bemused Mac Duff who laughed heartily yelled.

"You punks; haven't seen nothing yet!"

Slowed down; pointed to the remains of several late model Fords and Pontiacs, piled up and scattered inside two long narrow sheer ravines, one either side of the track hundreds of feet below. Mac Duff nearly home cackled, flashed his fang cracked up.

"Owned by God damn miners full of redeye; wrecked on their way to or from Dolly China's Brothel."

Suddenly out of utter silence the blunt nosed bruised Chevrolet thrust itself between two fully registered and guaranteed toxic phallic peaks, crude geophysical and intense human activity. Then stopped, up front and spread-eagled up was a towering crude timber structure, straddled by muscular bare chested men who heaved axes or large sledge hammers.

Michael Stockdale

The trucks passage impeded by competitive fast moving heavy haul trucks; demanded respect continually reversed and dropped rubble. Clattered bang on the top of more inclined abysmally constructed timber frames, and more men suspended with highly efficient compactors. This was the 24/7 Mine Bull Gang. Inside one week, another crude but effective new road built by hand from timber and rubble.

Economically planned, meant nearly everyone worked and lived in Elsa's township at Keno Hill Mines. No sealed roads or obvious suburbs except for several superior Staff Alpine lodges, solid timber with high pitched roofs a tad further south away from the 'workings.' In the main the Mine appeared as a collection of ram-shackled sheds, low-set outlying office/assay buildings. The stack and roof of the Mine's Power Station sighted from behind a colossal mountain of coal. Its Company Store seemed to be the brightest building came with the compliments of Tennessee Ernie Ford. Main Office stood alone and aloof, completely separated from other buildings. It was a subdued Mac Duff when he pulled up, discharged its contents then abruptly cleared off. Tomorrow he would pick up another bunch of broke migrant punks dragged off Edmonton's streets.

Reception at Main Office peered out towards ominous Death Valley, to its rear and far beyond an indistinct, vast canopy of black jagged mountains disappeared beneath thick layers of inanimate clouds. But once inside Main Office, staff dressed conventionally. Men wore conservative white stiff collared shirts and mediocre ties, aged ladies white hand stitched formal blouses; stout practical shoes. Doug signed on and was allocated quarters. His two pals soon on their way to another mine called Calumet said brief farewells and vanished. Doug was issued with two grey woolen blankets plus makeshift key to one basic room. He had no idea what to expect.

Guided by a tight mouthed indifferent Clerk he was allocated a shared room inside a dimly lit long narrow row of shallow huts called "The Ritz," stuck on the side of a steep rocky outcrop interlocked by crude wooden stairs. Room 22 was sparse more like a prison cell, two iron framed bunks, parked either side of a small screened window. No cupboards or drawers. No wardrobes just one five inch galvanized nail on each side of the door that was it. Home sweet home it was not. Dumbstruck he dumped his bags turned almost rigid and returned to Main Office stiff with rage said nothing.

With no formality the new Power Station man was told by Personnel he would start work the following day on days. Eight hours three separate alternative shifts, afternoons and nights. Signed and gave permission to the Pay Master to deduct monies from his fortnightly pay. To repay his transportation costs all the way from Gumption's Black Horse Hotel. Sing Hallelujah, he felt like a criminal. He had forfeited his passport in exchange for Cell 22 that came with a job. His day rate started at $1.90 per hour, afternoon and night shifts paid higher hourly rates. Shifts changed each week, tomorrow he would start on days, then afternoons and then on nights, seven days a week, thanks a lot Fergus McCloud. His quarters faced something referred to as Death Valley but he did not know why. In a matter of days it would be redefined as the Mine's tailings pond or where toxic waste from the separation of lead, zinc and silver was dumped. He returned to Room 22 now aware fifty paces from his bunk swung a suspended ore tramline. Located directly above "The Ritz" exit door it too operated 24/7.

Later that day he ate in the Mess, ran by genuine Chinese artifacts in pigtails, lads who apparently worked all day and gambled all night, or if broke slaved inside the mine's Chinese Laundry; cash only read the sign. Inside the Mess and above its long stainless steel food counter a large sign said "Only English May Be Spoken Here," yet the Chinese crew who cooked and served up grub only spoke Chinese.

That night Doug slept fitfully; dreamt he was somewhere else close to heaven when suddenly his face was drenched by a pungent familiar liquid. He shot up from his metal bunk. Choked and grabbed the bearlike figure that shrugged him off, missed the window once again with his senile dick and nearly drowned an innocent man. This human bear weighed a ton, was immovable and could barely stand, genuinely shocked to find his cave had been taken by another. Twenty stone of gristle, stammered profusely in gibberish perhaps the local Priest, boomed in impeccable English.

"Holy Mary Mother of God Please Forgive Me. Jesus Christ and his twelve disciples, please help me."

Pushed the panicked punk to one side easily, stumbled out and vanished. By now short of territorial logic Doug convinced half of Scotland had moved to Canada, his startled intruder the unicorn man, I come in peace drunkard articulate Mick McKee, the half beast half man who shared his room. He was the grotesque image of Basil, formerly of St. Egbert's

Tales from Planet Gumption

Church and later Bishop of Carlisle Cathedral.

It never happened again, Doug would rarely see McKee. Sometimes guised as a migrating whale he left fruit or some cake near his bunk, the local drunk he did not need and demanded another room or would leave. Contacted God; an alleged high ranking Mason by his handshake, sleight of hand at dominos and a sheer waste of time.

"Now then young man, what kind of threat was that, surrounded by utter desolation, Russian fur hats, mothballed Sputnik's further north but never on foot, no money in your pocket where would or could you go?"

Purdy the Timber-man a very close pal of McKee's, shared a room with another pal who had just left and offered his bunk to the dissolute punk.

Purdy's room was fully equipped with almost everything except the Holy Bible and rosary. Highly experienced with isolation Purdy stayed dry for six months at a stretch, thought it would do until the kid settled in. The first thing Purdy said to the kid was brief. Everything in his room was his to use and shared. Whipped out his wallet, knew he was broke and suggested a $25.00 loan.

"Go buy yourself a coffee down at the Mine coffee shop punk. Play chess, read a book, find and meet some new pals."

Purdy was another mountain of a man; partially deaf, blessed with a very loud voice called out "Hi-Ball," to everyone he met: Was stationed in London during WW2. Recounted how during Blackouts he would take his rifle climb on the roof, and if he saw a light shoot it out. He had two close pals at the Mine, McKee the punk had already met and the other an underground Miner. Calder was his name, carried a Black Belt in Martial Arts rolled cigarettes and would eventually become a close pal of his.

Jet propelled within twenty-four hours Doug's premature induction to Keno Hill tightened his belt. He had aged visibly. On his first day at the "Office," he smelled strongly of industrial disinfectant. Faced off Crazy Joe Keller's cold expressionless eyes the man he would replace at the Mine Power Station. The ex-German Army Corporal already packed to leave on three months furlough possessed a refined but cruel face. The kraut was overly friendly and carried a Derringer: Ominously spun around one index finger at the end of each sentence. Held it high and fired off a round. Grinned openly at Doug's knee jerk reaction and entered his domain in the shadow of a glittering, moist black coal stockpile. Got technical and informed him that coal stockpiles rested at 37 degrees except in wet weather. But had no idea how much coal was in the stockpile.

It was a brief introduction of the overall operation of the plant as by now a shaken Doug hastily took notes. Joe explained what was expected on each separate shift and how duties varied on all three. The main priority was to ALWAYS keep the coal bunker full. Before he left he asked Doug his age.

"Twenty three," his replacement spluttered.

"*Twenty-fucking' three?*" hissed Keller. "You know shit; you know fuck all, you know nothing. You're nothing but a young punk."

Kicked a rock as hard as he could; fired another round into the ground. Shook his head from side to side, bared his teeth and walked away disgusted.

The Mine Power Station operated two locomotive water-tube boilers fired by coal from the coal bunker and two electrode boilers normally placed on standby. Coal was fed to the boilers by gravity/or others, topped up manually by wheelbarrow, taken from a large coal stockpile situated on a steep hill outside and to the rear. The young punk watched on when Keller demonstrated what was expected. Then it was his turn. The world was mad inside his head crisscrossed when translated with Crazy Joe's garbled broken English instructions.

"Run up the hill with the wheelbarrow, grab the pick, break the coal it'll be sometimes frozen. Cast off the pick, grab that shovel and fill the wheelbarrow to overflowing. Turn around then run like hell back down to the bunkers and dump it."

The punk was by nature competitive. But not today completed the task at a much slower rate than Keller. Crazy Joe's one act of kindness was when he said.

"Sign up with the Company Store buy some vacuum boots and leather gloves, because the Power Station's appetite on all shifts was one ton of coal Herr Kiddo and bunkers must be fully topped up at all shift changeovers in all weathers."

Michael Stockdale

Doug was no mathematician. He estimated his angled climb was sixty yards and his total run one hundred and twenty yards. Now he knew why Crazy Joe was made from solid gristle without one inch of fat. Hands hardened shaped like dinner plates that bruised his fingers when they shook hands on their first meeting. This Yukon warm up would prove a serious challenge to the punk's physical condition but not his sanity. The full quid he once thought he was had become a distant memory.

The punk with no name as yet would later meet his two other 'colleagues.' One a short heavy built genial Italian called Marco and another squinty eyed German called Henri, an embittered ex WW2 veteran he sensed he would need to monitor. The Company Store sold almost everything and extended credit docked each month from their pay. The punk kicked it off with a pair of heavy leather gloves and a fine pair of insulated boots. He did not drink or smoke but required on the odd occasion the company of women. But as most of the ladies who worked there were either elderly, maligned widows or married with defeated expressions, he would have to wait. But right then he had two options, hitch a ride to Dawson or visit the local Indian reservation.

But he did not bother, finally settled into his new occupation and adapted to his new surrounds. His work on shifts seven days a week kept him fully occupied and was sacrosanct. His sleep was vital. He had also discovered it was a cardinal sin to disturb the sleep of any shift worker, particularly one who worked in the Mine Power Station. But he did have a company of sorts. It was something he had carried on all of his journeys. An old friend from the past that cheered him up, a reliable

Tales from Planet Gumption

harmonica he played when alone.

The punk as a kid and as an apprentice Fitter was always known as Doug; rarely Douglas. In the Merchant Navy first names were not acceptable when addressing an officer; Mr. Warrington, preferred when told what to do; plain WTF Warrington when out of step. At Keno Hill he would be the Limey or the young punk who played harmonica; the same 'God damn tunes' every day.

Time went quickly and his new Post Office savings account contained cash. He had acquired a few pals about his age, mainly Canadians. Two others were young aggressive Danish lads who picked fights specifically with Germans and one was a mad Hungarian lad who flew off to Edmonton to buy a big American limousine. On his return joined Keno's Limited Membership Ravine Club tanked up with Red-eye, seen parked alongside twelve other fine investments never to be driven again. Purdy had gone on furlough, his room booked when he returned and pal Calder moved in short term to protect his space.

In that wild not yet tamed Yukon Territory a man's life was his own business. Doug knew little about his friends other than they shared what they had and gave generously. Calder claimed he himself was a long time loser. The ultimate Joker rolled hand-made cigarettes at dawn, his interests too many stuff-ups failed Bank holdups no dough. Party man Purdy was known far and wide. Rented rooms in the biggest hotel in some distant town, filled with cornflakes drove an eight dog sled through low rental foyers pulled by huskies. McKee once struck it rich lost at Black Jack in one small smoke filled back room to the Mayor of

Michael Stockdale

Whitehorse. The story goes the Mayor held up the game and skid-addled back to Whitehorse for more funds. Caught his wife in bed with another and shot them both; returned to Keno to finish the game. Did not kill his wife or lover, when he returned to Whitehorse they had cleared off to Mexico.

Purdy, McKee & Calder were permanent fixtures in the Mine. They knew most of the Mine's characters, including Black Mike who lived in a hole in the ground outside of camp and invited Calder and Doug to dinner one day. Black Mike lived with Yorkshire Doris. A Manchester man on the run from an NW3 London robbery gone wrong lived underground on the cheap. Both ensconced beneath flattened out jerry cans, huge sods of earth. Carpet an underground spotless dirt floor it's décor; pink paper flowers kept inside a Staffordshire china vase. Their meal; always roast beef, roast potatoes and Yorkshire pudding. The spuds would be as hard as rocks, meat tough as teak but Doris's Yorkshire pudding came out top. Full of redeye they ate the lot. Doris suffered from a bronchial bad cough; convinced one more bad winter could kill her. But no one complained about anything inside their cave, their old settee a fixture made from real Italian leather, stained by unsteady guests who fell asleep; blamed Mike's bootleg liquor.

One day Calder suggested they should take a short walk, he had to be kidding, to visit an old Yukon ghost town called Keno City. Calder told him it was once a booming mining town mostly owned by a famous prostitute who still lived there and dreamt of unsteady happy times. But the best part was its Pub, untouched authentic snake rooms, no windows just one bunk. Barren cells adorned with ancient scriptures, one allegedly signed by celebrity Chef Ben Nevis where he and other sentenced booze riddled drunks had slept it off. Behind its magnificent Bar was a sign: "One hundred dollars to the man who could drink one tot from each bottle behind the Bar inside a specified time." But, before the game commenced the challenger placed one hundred dollars on the Bar and if they failed, it was pocketed by the Bar. Purdy was the only man known to win that prize, his Champion pint glass on display, tested every six months when he returned or before he went away.

There was no toilet or shower in the Power Station. No provision for the storage of personal items, and very little company either. When the punk needed a crap he did it behind the boilers on a solid piece of paper. It was a solitary, dirty, arduous lonely occupation and at times he felt a little sorry for himself especially when on nightshift. On cold nights he would wrap old rags round his wrists and ankles. Grabbed some shuteye curled up on a short padded ledge and never fell from it once. Sometimes, when on nightshift he would hear the grunts and movements of grizzlies amongst the timber but never saw them. But now and again one would fall on power lines and create instant power shortages. At some stage he constructed his own simple laundry; one half filled with water five gallon drum connected to a length of rubber hose. Its other end clamped to a boiler blow down valve. His washing powder generally was a small bar of soap sliced in pieces, dropped inside the drum and within half an hour produced alien soap bubbles.

Now and again he would have visitors. Two ancient slow talking Yankee prospectors who still worked at their own licensed 'diggings'; hacked out by hand and it showed. Then in their eighties, the two good

Michael Stockdale

old Tennessee boys knew every film John Wayne ever made, married girls from the Isle of Skye. Long since passed away; smoked clipped hand-rolled cigarettes, cigarette ash stored inside three inch denim turn ups and never once stubbed out butts.

Buck the shorter of the two, would roll in around midnight and park on Doug's padded seat with much the same old joke.

"Hey Doug, how yah doing, saw me some bars about two hours ago and I've brought you some moose to test out yah teeth?"

Ace's large triangulated skin and bone frame not far behind. He was the lay Preacher man who spoke of the devil; carried his Bible over his heart inside a padded bullet proof pocket. Spoke of the evils of drink and of the wild women who had led him astray. Each possessed standard Yukon shovel like hands, finger nails covered with gristle.

Both men were deeply religious and one day invited Doug when on day-shift to the Mine's small log cabin church. More out of curiosity he agreed to join them. The three men represented the entire congregation; two original old timers with no expectations and one greenhorn along for the ride. It was a pleasant enough non-denominational service, with a bleak view of Death Valley outside. They sang or mimed hymns, listened to the man in the dog collar, whiskers, long white hair and chatted a while about life in general.

By now Doug had read Voltaire, poems by Omar Khayyam, Robert Service and Walt Whitman the half man. Found in Purdy's collection of books; or anything that came to hand, his job deemed it. He had accepted his job as the only one in the Mine which demanded a seven day week; with very little or no time to socialize. A tad down at the mouth he came across an old Scottish newspaper he had found stuffed behind the desk in the Power Station. Inside were some cartoon characters drawn by Dudley D. Watkins entitled 'The Brown's' based on some crazy Scottish family and always in trouble. Then on another page, he came across the tragic story of a Glaswegian fallen on very hard times, which made his situation look kind of rosy.

So Doug decided to keep himself busy and occupied himself with the Plant's mechanical devices with the idea of improving their efficiency. Ironically, he had also discovered he was the only 'registered' Steam Plant Engineer in the Mine but thought it prudent not to display his maligned 'certificate.' Best left alone inside a hessian bag; Keno Hill was a world of its own.

One day Black Mike gave Doug a hinged lidded small wooden barrel. Said it could be a handy device to use as a cupboard to store snacks or spare pair of gloves. Doug attached to the wall near the Power Station exit. Curiously, it vanished within twenty-four hours. When questioned, an unhinged Henri denied any involvement, but logistics suggested he was a liar. Freaked out, Doug climbed down the rear of the Power Station and searched alongside the odious edge of Death Valley. Found his barrel covered in shit and shattered; climbed back and ripped Henri's padlocked four foot timber cupboard off the Station wall. Lifted it high above his head and threw it as far as he could down towards Death Valley. Watched it bounce and smash wide open, its contents scattered.

Michael Stockdale

Doug could not recall the exact time he was fronted, then questioned and threatened by Henri about his locker, outside the Mess. Lied and claimed ignorance, laughed it off time for chow.

"Fuck knows where you're bastard cupboard is or its contents."

Soon sly experienced ex-prison Warden Henri retrieved his possessions, but like Doug's barrel his cupboard too was dead. But the naive Limey had crossed a violent man with a lurid reputation. Spotted next day armed with a rifle backed away from the stockpile, slung low pointed in Doug's direction. His situation now looked decidedly grim. The idea of being shot over an inane act of juvenile retribution seemed bizarre. He now saw himself as stupid as the idiot man Henri, caught up in a B class Western melodrama, except this was real. There was no Stan the Man or off-sider Terrance the Menace to call on as in Gumption. Aye! Both good pals back home but nothing but tadpoles in this environment. But slow off the mark Douglas V for Victor Warrington was no longer the man he thought was. He had changed dramatically physically and mentally without knowing, hardened up slept like a baby.

Well, the word must have got around that the Limey punk was a dead man, because instead of eating alone he was joined by Calder unasked and two burly pals of his. Muttered they were there to watch his back. The nearest 'Police Station' was in Whitehorse a million miles away, and their seldom seen lone Mountie serviced an area bigger than Britain. On the outskirts of the Mine lived a large German community, its occupants mainly WW2 war veterans who just like Henri carried guns. Doug's pals

Tales from Planet Gumption

had plenty to worry about.

It must have been Sunday the day when most miners rested, ate roast turkey for dinner. The Mess fairly packed, when suddenly it went from a cheerful buzz to utter silence so obvious it could be cut by a cleaver. Calder recognized the unwieldy shape of the brute when he entered stiffened visibly gasped, "God-damn!" It was the last thing he expected to see, an apparition of the Yukon's mythical Wendi go; known as the Calumet Animal.

Calder nodded his head towards the punk, rose slowly to his feet gently exhaled, shirt knotted soaked in sweat. The punk seated; his torso fronted the Mess main exit, did not move or turn his head. He had seen far too many Westerns at Gumption's Regal Cinema. The throb from his heart said it was normal. Not one word exchanged or spoken. Chairs scraped against the concrete floor as the Animal nimbly glided closer and closer.

A gentle hand shook the punk's shoulder, the 'Animal's' huge battered but very welcome mug widened with a relieved grin. It was Heinrich the giant German miner he had travelled with by plane. The same man he had bought a beer with his last five bucks in Whitehorse not so long ago. Just in from Calumet, further north, when he had heard the drum. On a mission once the word had got around. He remained against their table one mighty hand encased the Limey's shoulder. Turned and faced the pensive crowded Mess growled in German and then in English.

Michael Stockdale

"This man Doug is my very good friend."

Only when everyone started talking eating, did he join them for a yarn. His English had improved, he had saved another dollar, and Karl was well, engaged to a Dusseldorf girl. Heinrich's parting shot was evil: Enough to compel Henri to change his ways withdraw, install new storage cupboards at his own cost. From then on and when in the Mess Doug's table became the focus of misappropriated punks and his social life improved but only marginally.

Sundays were days off for miners when only Doug, Marco and Henri worked shifts while Calder and Johnny Sheffield hung out at room 22, still obsessed with shady Bank holdups, their route to Mexico, best getaway cars ideally Skinny Adolf as driver. Estimated costs one thousand bucks the magic figure or enough to stake out Bank Britannia. Doug did not listen or take much notice; his main concern was the shortage of chicks. Jake the Mine's albino electrician was shacked up with two Squaws, cultivated yellow balls seen in the shower: The "Ritz' toilets and showers had no doors. Long shits attracted audiences and if they really smelled, loud complaints about diet and lack of privacy.

One evening Doug's sleep was broken by a violent, explosive brawl in the corridor outside, loud curses and violent blows. The thud of mortal combat, wild cries of anguish against thin fibro walls and vague omnipresent childlike whimpers. Doug stepped out to intervene to stop the racket. In the shadows and to his left the tall young punk he knew as the kid from out of town. In one hand held a long Bowie knife his other arm protected by thick denim, his enraged opponent Radio Dave from

Tales from Planet Gumption

the room opposite.

"You're done for you slimy piece of shit," cried the kid, stepped forward lunged the knife.

"Fuck you," snarled Dave unleashed his buckled belt with tethered razor blades.

"Fuck you both," shouted Doug and faced them off. "You know the rules. I'm on shifts and need some shuteye. Bugger off and take you're fight outside."

They stopped, Dave relieved apologized, both skid-addled and recommenced outside in Tramline Alley. It was an unwritten law not to disturb shift workers and punishable offence: Minimum penalty, a Mine initiative, fourteen days 12 hours per day hard labor, half pay in the Mine's Bull Gang. Doug watched them leave and was about to close his door noticed Radio Dave's still open. Doug spied two much younger kids either semi-conscious or half asleep sprawled across Dave's mattress.

In those days Doug knew little about drugs and pedophiles or Dave's heroin addiction. He only knew him as Radio Dave who worked in the Mine Assay Office, or heard part time on the Mine's radio station. The trail of blood in the corridor next day led and stopped at Dave's door. The kid from out of town had sliced him; the two younger kids had vanished. Rumor had it the out of town kid was there to protect his younger brother and to do Dave in for good.

Michael Stockdale

It might have been the day when Doug heard from dear Agnes and in detail all about her new Romeo, Stan the Barber or when he sensed some connection at the Company Store. The misshapen lump wore no makeup, disguised by a long white coat that doubled as brush and scraped the floor. Hair well concealed beneath a savage canvas cap, clumped around in standard safety boots. Two bright green eyes, rarely smiled or showed her teeth, pushed aside by Maggie May, the school-bus driver's wizened wife with her well-honed greeting.

"Hi there honey, how's my old hound Doug today?"

Then again one week later swore he heard young female laughter from the Store's backroom. Approached his Stiffness, Angus the Store Manager, who advised in a winsome manner they were the sounds of female relatives of Senior Staff, final year University Students on vacation. An annual Mine special occasion celebrated with an official Ball inside the Mine's private function rooms: Black tie, fancy grub, free booze, an imported live band behind closed doors and by invitation only.

Doug attracted older women and almost knew it. Passed by Coffee Shop; imagined legs ahoy inside the only decent legs for two hundred miles. Walked on! His only other port of call was Elsa's Post Office, pick up his mail and chat with Willie the Postmaster. Usually, "Dear son," guarded hand written letters from his reliable Dad; news of inclement weather and the terrible state of Gumption's darts team. PS. 'Seventy five job opportunities at the Shipyard.' Agnes wrote and declined his offer to shack up next door to Black Mike and Yorkshire Doris. Said her Dad had sold his Funeral business and moved in with

Tales from Planet Gumption

another woman known as twice on Wednesday.

Willy the Postmaster was a stocky Geordie Newcastle born and bred. Liked a joke passed on old newspapers from home. Today as usual he greeted Doug with his thick Geordie banter,

"Hey hinny, Maggie May fancies you. Heard tell she calls you Hound Doug these days. How's the howling going? What've yah been up to pal? Still fighting WW2?"

"Nothing much old son," egged Doug. "Hear tell there's a bit action about."

"Aye, you'll be right about that hinny. I'll tell yah best show in town it is. By the way there's no overseas mail today son."

"OK, I'll be off then. Keep us posted." Doug turned to make room for Willy's customers, but the Geordie called him back.

"Aye, well there's no mail from home, but I do have something for yah."

Produced a small blue envelope with local stamp, Doug studied closely and saw his name D.V. Warrington. C/O Elsa Post Office, Yukon Territory: Printed formally not by hand but by typewriter.

"Yah going to open it?" queried Willy.

Michael Stockdale

Mail, any mail, all mail Doug treated carefully, peeled the envelope slowly open. Not fast enough for impatient Willie or the extended queue now gathered outside his tiny Post Office cried,

"For Christ's Sake open the bloody envelope man."

"What's this?" gasped Doug. "It's a bloody invitation to the do. Look at this Willie. Hey man it's a bloody invitation. Wow!" Doug, still unaware of his audience, waved the inscribed invitation high in the air and disappeared in a cloud of dust.

One of Mine's 24/7 coalmen; nose perennially blocked with coal dust, throat thick with phlegm could not believe his eyes. What should or could he wear? He only had one suit, two shirts, one pair of heavy brogues and he could not find his tie. He had flogged the rest of the stuff in his last week in Edmonton. Convinced, his blue Kinnock Tweed full drape suit, fob pocket single breasted and vented rear flap was a bobby dazzler. To his mind it went well with stout heavy brogues. Short of a tie, he settled for a washed black shoe lace hung cowboy style from one of his work boots.

On the night of the Mine's show piece for the year Doug tagged along with another invitee Chinese Joe, a supercilious Junior Geologist. His intelligent Asian face framed by sharp large spectacles, made his eyes look twice the size. By comparison Wong wore a fine white cotton shirt, smart navy blue blazer, dark blue tie to match; neat dark grey strides and a pair of Church's suede's. His demeanor restrained, but behind that expressionless innocent face lurked a very hot temper indeed. Do not

Tales from Planet Gumption

mess with him. He led the way to the rear of Main Office to a large double doorway already festooned with streamers and balloons; policed by two senior clerks in evening dress. They flashed their invitations and entered what appeared to be an endless large polished hardwood paneled room full of swaying bodies where some, possibly students wore fancy dress.

Stunned to see Willy the Postmaster tonight's Barman; haplessly drunk in fine fettle. Doug wandered around with Chinese Joe until they found seats. Meanwhile perhaps a glimpse of something special in the company of Jack, Keno's young Doctor, fooling about showing her off. Spun her around and around in the center of the floor; created chaos a huge grin on his face. All eyes focused on his partner fancy dressed in school uniform. Mini-skirted, old school straw boater, fine pair of sexy legs clad in black fishnet tights. Whoa Trigger! Douglas V for Victor Warrington was back on familiar territory Gumption's bawdy Saturday night dances. Aye! Did he know this chick? Hang-on her face looked familiar, perhaps one he had seen at a distance in the Coffee Shop? In a way she reminded him of Agnes in her hay day. Oozed confidence, a wonderful body not seen or held since he had left Prospect in a hurry. Engrossed, it never dawned on him they would soon be dancing cheek to cheek. When suddenly Doc waltzed close to where he sat, winked one eye strolled over with this mix of Christie/Bardot green eyed beauty her arm linked inside his, and faced Doug with a grin.

"It's you," gasped Doug and rose clumsily to his feet.

"Hello sailor! Call me Chantilly let's dance honey."

Michael Stockdale

Doug had not held a woman in his arms since half past eight do not be late down a Keswick back street. But tonight, the unexpected metamorphosis of the Store's misshapen lump to that of showgirl Chantilly stopped him in his tracks. Still unaware she had been attracted to him the moment she heard his accent. Two peas in a pod, both from similar backgrounds her Geordie Dad and his step-son Doc were Newcastle born and bred. Her Dad had sailed for Shell and now was into mining. Doug's RMS Queen Mary role had impacted. Few mariners sailed Keno's streets. Those envisaged reservations held by Doug she demolished within seconds.

Germaine, Germaine his hometown nemesis: The dying girl who toyed with emotions. Her play with words "I've met somebody else," the ultimate travesty. As on the night when he walked her home and she had fainted during a thunderstorm; lifted bodily scared stiff and carried to a nearby Bus Shelter. Held her tight until she came round sobbed in his arms. She knew then as did her parents she was dying but never told him. Tired with the ongoing drama he gave her the flick and dated Banana girl, his viable substitute. Time passed. Germaine down from College crossed Doug's path and baled him up. Looked great and invited him to a party in Runner's Park. Now a man of means he picked her up in his fifty quid, two-seater hill climb car outside her garden gate. Her smiling tiny mother dashed out of the house. Donated a bottle of cheap wine and waved them off until out of sight.

He had never owned a car, she seemed impressed. Placed one arm around him as he drove up Dalton Road whispered in his ear she would

Tales from Planet Gumption

go to Canada. Tight lipped he had said nothing until they reached the semi-detached floodlit house, the sounds of laughter and music, its inviting door wide open. He had dropped her off with a one liner.

"That's it pet, we're finished," drove away.

One year later her unexpected Xmas card, her London address and telephone number, 'she'd love to see him.' Tracked him down on board RMS Queen Mary when he believed she did not need or really want him or anyone, within six weeks her sudden death unnerved him: Idle Keno thoughts. He had figured it out and embraced Chantilly with fervor.

"THIS MAN HAS SAVED ONE THOUSAND BUCKS" yelled Willie the Postmaster to a more than interested queue inside his Post Office where security was low and 'Honey' did not know where to look. A few whistles perhaps a pat on the back acknowledged as he made it out. One thousand bucks was the agreed amount it took to rob an Edmonton Bank. His door rattled by "knock, knock," had caught the eye of local crooks. Well, at least for a while, then interest petered out.

Sometimes Doug wondered if he had learnt more about himself or more about others in his self-imposed exile. His job paid well during difficult times, the question was should he move on or stay exactly where he was? The Mine's ever active promotion cycle appeared to have some plans; their electrode boilers now worked better than before. His social life fitted in well in between shifts, and he rarely spent a bean. If the Mine closed down, many would stay where they were; no mortgage or rent and who needed a car? Service's lyrics tethered alongside London's

Michael Stockdale

Call of the Wild appealed to millions. His brand new world vastly different to the one he had left; he had seen more compassion in Keno than he had seen anywhere else. Elsa's United Vagabond Corporation never closed. Open twenty-four hours, seven days a week.

When it did not snow it rained a lot at Keno Hill, sometimes for days. Its vast hinterland layered as if by sodden Canteen tea towel clouds close enough to touch. The township's garbled radio waves picked up Russia; long tiresome tirades greeted by jeers. He rarely listened to still-alive Radio Dave's contribution, played his harmonica. 'The Rock island line,' was one of his favorite songs. Definitely preferred eggs 'on the turn', instead of scrambled. Jam with Oat meal porridge. Carnation Cream supplied by pals he drank to remove black coal dust from his lungs; an ongoing hazard. His long intimate walks with Chantilly; buttered with Whitman's woefully didactic poems never failed; careful not to walk too far because it was so easy to get lost. She made few demands if any. Then one evening sat alone he recalled when Crazy Joe Keller questioned his age on his first day at the 'office,' said 23. Was derisive, brushed it off.

"You know shit; you know fuck all, you know nothing. You're nothing but a young punk."

Shook his head from side to side then walked away on holidays. That single moment repeated itself the day before the punk was about to be married and weighed heavily. Maybe Joe was right. McCloud's derision was something else but in its way undeniably accurate. In twenty four hours a planned reception in Keno Hill's private function room after

Saturday's wedding in Elsa's tiny log cabin Church. Doug and Chantilly's bags already packed and labeled. Flights and hotel accommodation booked for a Caribbean honeymoon donated by his prospective in-laws.

He panicked and told Chantilly he could not do it and was leaving. She did not believe him, convinced he would still be there at the aisle and watched him edge slowly down the stock-pile. He turned to wave his last farewell and saw her wild diminutive figure bracketed against the North's ragged skyline.

He could not leave her, said "Fuck it."

Scaled the stockpile like a rabbit but arrived too late. She had vanished into a brief thick mist then sheeting rain.

Early morning, he too was gone.

The Hairdresser's Daughter

Two inch long gold fingernails tattooed shoulders Agnes Ripley sat alone on the last Abbey bus home. Stunned by NWEM's front page headline **"No Groom at the Top"** pushed Town Hall elections and Rugby League to back page. Displayed a photograph of Doug and Ms. Chantilly Lode, the only daughter of Maurice "Mother" Lode, Canadian Mining Mogul outside a Yukon Power Station; subtitled **"Too hot to handle."** Agnes nearly fainted. Gasped for air, stumbled at the terminus and swallowed a soluble Aspirin.

Michael Stockdale

Spring: "April in Portugal," played on every radio. Washed to his waist, Douglas V for Victor Warrington back in town stepped out of 123 Lord Street with no set plan. Open house; maybe travel to Ulverston and check out Coronation Hall. The town's only serious member of rural Facebook: Rustic, less ornate and much smaller than Gumption's Public Hall. Not far from eminent Plaxo Laboratories where kimono draped ripe banana girl worked as Lab technician, within sight of Grange over Sands and Morecambe Bay. No terra firma local muscle sighted on Windermere for weeks. "Skin Deep;" played repetitively as hard-wired farmer boys teamed up inside quaint Newby Bridge Hotel, played Darts and supped. Distant Drums as Gary Cooper's Trio played at sporadic Hunt Balls, held in modicum country village halls, "Oh my Papa" preferred by modicum bands as each three piece competed with Ulverston's Big band on Friday Nights.

Faraway from Ulpha's, Lindale's and Broughton's Hunt Balls ruled by local grenadiers, the Coro's crowd attracted mainly motley urban, past and present Miss Ulverston beauty queens. Stiff young things posed in corners dressed in overdone frilly dresses like courtiers at Buck Palace, melancholy out of touch middle income women who dreamt of Frank Sinatra. But not tonight bonny lass; glassy eyed, demure pony tailed Coniston Penny, solid gristle the only one missing. Somewhere else but still in town Dolly the Stag Hotel's austere barmaid going on fifty craved recognition. Accepted tips from fast Cavendish Eddie who panted; anxious for free out-of-town leg-overs. Tired old nags not much doing at Doug's end until he met a girl he did not know, out and about at her first real dance. Wide eyed, scheduled to be picked up by Dad at Tudor

Tales from Planet Gumption

Square, Dalton 10.30pm; deputized him to accompany her. Her lift parked outside Tudor Square's Bus Shelter in the shadows. Introduced him to her non- querulous Dad half asleep peered through the car's window; sized Doug up did not recognize said "How do;" lit a fag. Then just before they left, she lowered a window leaned out and unexpectedly invited Doug to tea.

"Say this Sunday about three, Low Hall, Burlington."

Drove off skid-addled, five minutes later puzzled Doug climbed aboard his packed Ribble bus full of drunks and headed back to Gumption.

Many years had passed since the man from Gumption last caught a red Dalton Ribble bus. Today he would get off at Hades. Several dinky toy terraced cottages each one indebted to millionaire views hunched together on the side of Kirkby Moor. Here he paused awhile. Inhaled burnt apple wood smoke from a roadman's fire waft from one of many multi-colored cracked chimney pots. Then watched a squadron of senile squawking crows in bold conversation chased away from someone's newly painted eaves. To the west and at sea level the brown murky Duddon Estuary snaked and stretched for miles, absorbed by vast lingering dangerous marshes. Sighted again the boxed steel bows of the never submerged Railway Bridge where he had fished as a child. East and inland, tipple down Marsh Side hamlet, dour Ulrich's house, steel-eyed, morose Tucker Hero's farm. Just and so southern placed Whelp's Head with its sugar like white sand. Further north prairie-like low set land, prone to floods that attracted varied bird-life. On its western side Cumberland's extinct volcano, shaped like a reclining woman, somnolent

Michael Stockdale

heavy breasted Black Combe. Its soft contours separated by the tidal Duddon that flooded marshes and sometimes covered low lying partitioned fields. Areas owned but rarely maintained by one or two slated, neglected farms, half dead or immobilized.

The road to Burlington was well maintained, protected and harbored by rambling moors. Doug estimated it would take him twenty minutes to somehow find her house. The bold sign read BURLINGTON erected at its boundary was typical of the area and the times. Tom Bones sang in St. Cuthbert's choir and rang its bells. Doug passed his small cottage, maybe tulips in the garden, where Tom's Dad once stood and spat; changed his mind when company present and swallowed. Transported back in time, when he stayed with his mother's relative's Alice and Royce Rolls a childless couple. Uncle Royce was the local Roadman, lost a leg in France and had lived in a small slate cottage at Wall Start.

The sound of metal against metal from Burlington's old Smithy resonated inside his head. Mesmerized by the heat and the roar from the furnace fire after he and Alice cycled up from Wall Start; watched the Smithy shape red hot horse shoes automatically; placed in orderly rows by the door. Children's shrill squeals when stung by sparks from its glowing embers; the hollow whistle from his well blackened bellows; old tools no longer used.

Burlington's village shop had not changed. Its shabby pennant still advertised Marsh's lemonade. Inside its main window a bank rolled selection of multicolored jars. Emblazoned with signs he had almost forgotten. Touted black rolls of Spanish, Mars bars, Cadbury's chocolates, menthol sweets, even Fisherman's Friend all kept in place by an ancient glass shaped polar bear; packed solid with Arctic Mints. To the rear on a wall a pre-WW2 poster of the Bisto Kids and a bold Wall's Ice Cream sign. Supplemented by an old but fashionable, chipped painted green large metal watering can. Placed inside, some pretty flowers shaped like a parasol.

Doug left the shop behind and followed a narrow two sided string of white washed terraced cottages, as the width of the road gave way to a narrow lane. Crowded in and overhead a mangled natural roof formed by two wild untrimmed hedges, thick with Rose hips, in earnest conversation. Then a break, a slice of sky the lad came across a gate. A large brass plate imprinted with Low Hall in fine Gothic print, when opened led to a crazed stone path fronted by a large ornamental garden. Groups of assorted apple trees, a graveled driveway headed and defined by a turning circle and not surprisingly a dog. It was a friendly Fox Terrier bitch, in fine fettle too. They played together for a while when the lad suddenly sensed someone close near at hand.

The girl smiled sheepishly said "Hi-yah," as she stepped out he recognized but in broad daylight looked younger than eighteen, not yet fully grown, tall and ungainly, small generous mouth; large buck teeth. She wore her long mousy colored hair carefully placed around her shoulders above her modest dress and yet when she took him by the hand, she giggled like a school girl. Arched her back as she guided her trophy up and through into her mock Tudor house via the kitchen, past an AGA cooker into a spacious lounge room and well setup table. Her name was Mavis Pricket, the only child of Albert Pricket he knew by sight. Albert the Tobacconist part time Hairdresser cut hair; smoked and sold cigarettes in his Cornwallis Street shop came with a hard core thick Gumption accent. Her mother Rita, another Hairdresser operated an up market Ladies Salon in Scott Street, both shops stayed open six days a week.

Albert was about as tall as him, extremely thin, and like most Barber's his ginger hair was thin on the top. But the eyes behind his rimless glasses twinkled mischievously when he shook the lad by the hand said "How-do Douglas." By contrast wife Rita had a strong masculine face, was heavy breasted, said it as it was. She looked liverish, pouched dark shadows beneath her eyes, wore corsets, iron bars by another name but made the lad feel at ease and completely at home. For a second they had forgotten their two other guests sat quietly to one side. The local Gumption sharp faced Magistrate dressed conservatively and his jolly rounded wife all floral, perceived by the girl's trophy as a strange enough combination when settled. Doug straight backed, cross-legged arms folded. On the defense prepared for cross examination.

They recognized from the article which first appeared in gossip magazine Star: Leapt upon by Gumption's NWEM because Editor Franklin Woods played Darts twice a week with Doug's Old Man. The hard faced Magistrate was sharp with it, the first to cross the line whined,

"Aren't you the lad who cleared off and stood this heiress woman up?"

Doug flinched. He had expected an inquisition. No one hereabouts runs away from brass. Floral Gloria, the Magistrate's buxom wife preened was coy,

"Said to be a Millionaire's daughter too? You would've been set up for life son."

Just like Agnes, they could not believe it. Not so the Magistrate who persisted further with a more incisive question,

"Was she pregnant?" Paused and fiddled with the Radio Times regained ground, "Oh I'm sorry son, such bad taste. Was she eh?"

"No she wasn't pregnant Squire and besides, my life has nothing to do we' you."

Climbed from his chair, he had heard enough. He did not take kindly to pointed questions from strangers. He was an independent young man who had probably done Chantilly a favor. Aged 23 he had not been ready for marriage.

"Well, I'll be off then. Thanks for supper. It was very nice meeting you all. Cheerio, I'll see my own way out."

They rose up from their chairs gradually, uncertain of what to say and groped self-consciously for clues a little surprised by Mavis's new friend's terse attitude. Rita ruffled and appalled by the rudeness of Magistrate Sydney Leopold Tight, the first to speak.

Michael Stockdale

"You'll not leave here young man until you've eaten further. Now please sit down and tell us all about the Yukon. And as for you Sid," her finger pointed at the magistrate,

"This is our house and not a Courtroom."

Then sat down, reclaimed their easy chairs and ate precision made red salmon sandwiches followed by the usual Madeira cake from delicate china plates as they watched Sunday Night at the Palladium on black & white TV. No one quizzed the lad about what he did for a crust or where he lived, the fact Doug was from Gumption they knew exactly where he was from. Said, "Aye," at the close of every sentence, already knew he had served his time as a Fitter at Pickersgill's: His present position was one of thousands who worked in the Shipyard and raised the ire of Mrs. Pricket who snapped.

"My father worked on a slot machine in the 'yard all his life. I'll have you know. Albert's favorite nephew is a Rate Fixer there and had got on. Had earned his stripes," nodded her head with approval.

"Aye, he's now Chief Rate Fixer in the Gun Shop."

Within half an hour Doug discovered he had stepped into a 'love' triangle. His 'date' now seated brazenly on his knees offered more Madeira cake, had fallen out with her status boyfriend and used Doug to make Cyril Prince jealous. Cyril was the son of soon to be Dockyard Manager, Philip Prince an important man in the Gumption. They lived in Hindpool's Garden of Eden a gardener's dream, inside another but real

Tales from Planet Gumption

mansion with a largely significant talked about walk-in freezer and bred race horses outside of Millom. Their Mansion overlooked Black Combe and Get it Sellafield round the corner and were acknowledged as local royalty. Grew real Peacock's instead of flowers, son Cyril rode to school on a scooter, the same school as the girl's. Their relationship was approved and encouraged by the new Hairdresser owners of Low Hall. With that in mind Doug accepted Mr. Pricket's offer to drive him home but only after they had all watched Sunday Playhouse on TV and another cup of tea.

Albert drove his far from modest gleaming automobile like the racing car it was, wore a sharp local cap, hand-made in Egremont. Slouched inside an expensively cut dogs toothed jacket, on his left wrist the glimmer from an old 22ct gold wristwatch. He smoked cigarettes and cracked jokes along the way. Asked the lad if he played cards and what his interests were. Already knew Doug would be in Scotland for six more weeks, and did not seem concerned. Dropped him at 123 Lord Street, said "Cheerio," wished him all the best spun his wheels and was on his way.

Pickersgill's most recent Government project based in Scotland was now Doug's second home. He had heard about it and the big money paid inside Gumption's Imperial Hotel during his first week back from Canada. The company required more tradesmen to work on the project. Douglas applied and was successful, but after three months confined to 72 hours per week, one fortnight about on nights found it boring and repetitive. Now topped up with Scottish notes in Barclay's Bank, added to the wad of cash he had saved in the Yukon he could buy outright a semi-detached Gumption house and perhaps his Grandmother's she had offered. But tucked away he had been impressed by his Gumption pals who had knuckled down, unlike him and completed their Engineering courses.

It was Saturday night in Wick; a Boxing Tent in town, Fidel Milano a Fitter on Site he knew from school was up against a local fighter. Doug paid the bag man, and joined the crowd of drunks. Surly body builder extraordinaire Fidel, hair carefully combed stood the better odds. But once his cultured muscles were on display; looked ponderous and slow, up against a wiry Scotsman who danced around the ring. The Scotsman full of spite; collided with the referee's head and they knocked each other out. Two drunken lads each one deprived of action; identified anyone as their target; sorted by two burly red faced policemen inside thirty seconds.

By now Doug at a very early age had seen the fossils on the dark side of the moon. Sailed the high seas as far as Scandinavia and survived a savage storm off Curacao on Fischer Tankers: Once hit a whale mid-ocean between Southampton and New York while serving on a famous British Liner. Seen the Yukon River flow and stood alone for hours inside Robert Service's Whitehorse log cabin. Thought of girls he had once known. Yet Chantilly remained an enigma. Unable to comprehend why he had contacted her on his last day in Edmonton. It may have been by association as he strolled out of curiosity through her old University grounds. Then the glimpse of a white stretch limousine, her inside agitated, flushed and overdressed stepped out. His anonymity lack of courage as he sidled away and hours later climbed aboard a BOAC

Tales from Planet Gumption

jetliner, their only passenger. His worldly route terminated via Heathrow and then Manchester, "Call of the Wild" as now he knew it was omitted as essential reading before or after puberty.

Behind his wooden desk in the early '50's at the Alf's, Mr. Ram his impatient English teacher died for a smoke, out of cigarettes, a failed bet at today's races, nothing bronchial tight cummerbund. But old enough to understand Conrad's nuanced layers inside his Heart of Darkness book, about those who sailed the sea. But Doug at sixteen, green around the gills, saw nothing except a glimmer. Early months at Punter's Yard, glib black toothed, aged grubby Frankie there on re-habilitation. Offered sixpence to retarded Joe to put his hand inside his shirt, then said it was a joke. His short compatriot crippled George who could not walk, angrily disapproved. Married to a prostitute, his crippled legs cured at a séance held at the Mason's Hall.

The Gun Shop's Marker-Off a short tubby man with a limp moustache reeked of perfume; minced along inside a belted pressed boiler suit worked a flanker with his assistant Alf. Lank Alf was his pet whippet, lean and hungry, another paper Mache macho man who wore braces and liked tartan caps. At first sight two congenial men or anybody's Uncles were treated lightly and not as two old men who plain and simple penetrated bums. They operated as a pair, but were awkward in their manner, their technique based on ridicule used up for conversation. They were viewed as entertaining, full of childlike banter, but when impassioned with a target, became aggressive with the kill. On the hunt around the workshops, time again for tea, then back off down the Docks, inside a darkened hulk. Both pursued young Store boys openly, mainly in or around the Gallery lift. Both worked for Fidel Milano's strange Head Foremen in the Gun Shop, freshly relocated on assignment in Scotland, a fundamental new addition to its new age management at the important, prestigious Pickersgill's high security Rapid Response Site.

Now and again Doug encountered this thick set suspect species Head Foreman, in the street or inside any local Pub when he bought up the bar. His communication technique was much the same as his two bum boys, banter garnished with ridicule, best ignored if a come on. The odds were that the long winded circular pinned on the Site Notice Board was his idea. All welcome to a Pickersgill's Private Function at the best Hotel in town, where management and employees could socialize, wear decent clothes and chew the fat awhile. The Hotel would provide the catering and drinks would be on the house, ensured a large number of attendees with a heavy thirst. It included local dignitaries, two wore chains but on the night and not unexpected most guests were reeling men.

Doug rarely drank but went along to wave the flag. Joined and mixed with mainly a middle aged, orderly crowd, but no talent about soon called it a day. The exit between the two Bars was narrow; blocked by the suspect Head Foreman and another Manager he did not know. The same old thrusting banter, now face to face but too close for him. No wish to get involved in a fight with management as an audience looked on; he pushed forcibly past both men and headed off to reception. Picked up his coat and paid the cloakroom attendant when a hand from behind grabbed his shoulder. WTF Head Foreman the man he did not know and did not want to know, he clouted hard and fast. His assailant's face badly

Tales from Planet Gumption

broken, a well bloodied mess screamed and fell heavily to the floor. The Hotel's astute Manager was on duty at reception and an instant witness. But instead of protecting Doug went to the aid of his assailant. His frantic, outstretched fingers clawed at Doug's face; snapped some broken, screamed to an empty reception.

"Phone the bloody Police."

His cry ignored by two Foster Wheeler welders who had followed Doug, stepped in and said nothing grabbed and whisked the lad out through the Hotel's rear exit.

It only seemed like only yesterday when he was coerced to take compassionate leave by the paternal stewardship of RMS Queen Mary and tried out Canada. Gambled it would be enlightening to be met by wafer thin platitudes from Albertan McCloud. His ridicule and inane laughter; classified and written off by an official Albertan Steam Engineer's Certificate which emphasized its lack of value with "…Subject to qualifications." The bleak desolation of Keno Hill Mines when he arrived and where he had bit the bullet and shifted one ton of coal by hand in all weathers. Worked night and day seven days a week and passed the test at Keno Hill. Beneath the Arctic Circle where men slaved and straddled huge timber logs as fifty ton trucks endlessly dumped rubble. Cast in stone no change in his soft spot for his boarding house Church Street Grandmother; always supplied her with duty free cigarettes, when on leave or on the run. Ate her iron hard Eccles cakes as if still fresh, with the knowledge they were more than six weeks old, kept inside a floral not so air tight tin she kept handy in a drawer.

Michael Stockdale

When Doug walked into the Site Mess the day after his much publicized fracas it was unusually quiet, no how's your father chat? Just casual nods, knowing winks from shift workers and union officials who waited for the outcome. But the expected call from Site Management did not happen. No reprimand followed. He was not sacked it was imagined; nothing happened. Yet the lad sensed it would be noted perhaps in long hand by Personnel back in Gumption recorded in a greasy book, stuck on a dusty shelf for reference and posterity.

The Site's pale young educated Manager sat bolt upright behind his tidy desk; his grey racing man's trilby hat firmly affixed; sported a tweed double breasted overcoat, red waistcoat and conservative dark grey trousers; startling yellow Cape Buffalo brogues. Waved his pasty white hand called out,

"Take a chair son. What's all this nonsense about you resigning Douglas, don't you like it here? Why would anyone want to leave a substantially paid occupation?"

Leaned back in his chair and waited for an answer.

"I'm going to enroll at Gumption's College of Technology and complete my Engineering studies," blurted Doug.

His answer totally unexpected, the Site Manager more than relieved. He did not need formal complaints about senior management or the possibility of subsequent strike action. He had enough on his plate as it was. Laughed it off, leaned across his desk, outstretched his hand and conceded the lad's plan had merit.

Railway Stations can be lonely places if they do not have a Cafeteria. Doug had already said his farewells to the Gumption boys and would no doubt catch up with some of them as usual in Dalton Road. Relaxed, he had not noticed another person stood to one side in the shade with a large suitcase at her feet. He recognized, and called out.

"Hey. Jean!" Then up and walked towards her.

"Is it Doug?" She jumped as she recognized his voice, "It's good to see yah bonny lad."

They embraced but more as pals and not as lovers.

"You're off then? You finally made it, so what's the story?"

He was really pleased to see her. Grabbed her suitcase, winked an eye into her flushed excited face.

"We'll sit awhile close by and you can bring me up to date."

Jean was the girl Doug had walked home some weeks earlier after a dance and shared her supper before he left. Unemployed and only eighteen, she was a burly attractive girl. He recalled in detail the night he had sat inside her parent's miserable kitchen; the lank taped joints between the walls and ceiling. Her entire 'home' was taped like a cardboard box by nothing more than two inch masking tape and tacks. She had insisted that he should join her for supper. Doug had sensed some guilt in sharing her precious two boiled eggs, bread, margarine, two mugs of strong tea and unnecessary paper napkins. They had spent an hour and talked about work opportunities, her unemployed parents and her failure to find work. But today she was excited, vocal and cracked jokes. She had applied for and had been accepted for a clerical role in the Army; headed south to some English Barracks. She wore a pastel yellow cotton two piece, shoes to match never worn at any dance. They travelled together as far as Glasgow, and celebrated in the dining car until someone chased them out. To the tune of Scotland the Brave's railway wheels as they trundled alongside Gulf Stream currents, was that Ben Hope? Soon the Lowlands came into sight then boldly grim shabby never sober strident Glasgow.

He watched her step lightly down the platform, pause and wave then disappear. Minutes later he was taken aback by the tap of a truncheon on his table: The sound of a guttural impatient voice,

"Hey! Finish that drink or leave it Jimmy."

It came from the bellicose Policeman at six o clock as he closed down Glasgow's Station Bar. Inside Doug's heavy brogues forty crushed Scottish pounds for emergencies.

It was his suave brother Joe dressed to the nines who met him at Gumption's Railway Station then strolled back to 123 Lord Street. Next day sharpish, found Doug outside the Shipyard's gates then inside to

Tales from Planet Gumption

seek a job. His best bet was the Engine Shop Extension where he had once worked as an apprentice. Its tall white haired bespectacled smock attired Foreman remembered him favorably and possessed an empty lathe. Located behind silent Bob who always smelt of last night's beer he knew. In front of massive Jack, a distant admirer of his Grandmother; smoked a pipe all day long and dribbled down past several chins. Two weeks about on shifts. His Foreman's last words

"Start next week and don't be late, good to see you son."

Part A of his plan was now completed and he walked down to Gumption's College of Technology and enrolled for Part B, his Engineering courses. Evening classes started in twelve days. Commenced at 6.00pm until 9.00pm, four nights a week; ideally suited for his night shift start up 10.00pm; completed when the hooter blew at 7.30am.

It was his first shift on nights, stomach rumbling and fatigued, Doug walked slowly through the Shipyard's workshops towards the grey exit. Straight between its large wrought iron gates swung wide open, through and against the incoming black tide back to No123.

His Grandmother in working attire, her usual pinafore had been pleased to see him and his wallet. She offered again to sell him her Church Street house for two hundred and fifty quid provided she could live there free. It was a generous offer, but being young he did not see the bargain. Had he been ten years wiser he would have bought it straight away. Her house had over twenty rooms, if converted into several flats he would have owned an investment for life with some change still in his pocket.

The self-induced shift worker from No123 now operated a lathe and attended night-school four nights per week; met up again with the Burlington lass and her hospitable parents. He discovered she rode horses in Gymkhana's, her mounts provided by someone else. A Lancaster carpet wholesaler, his wife a flirt and good dancer, her husband's horses considered the best.

Sydney the sharp faced Magistrate full of gossip and wife Gloria still came around for tea. Both knew Doug flattened Head Buffalo Man in Scotland when Sydney brought up the subject with Albert.

"I don't know about this lad Warrington and you're Mavis."

"I know all about it Sid," replied Albert with a grin, "He's not the problem but Cyril Belcher and his band is and you know exactly what I mean. Why your secret handshake lot, cover for him beats me? C'mon let's join the ladies. If we don't go now they'll get suspicious and think we're drinking whiskey instead of tea."

These weekend soirees occurred alternate weekends when the Pricket's visited Mr. and Mrs. Sydney Leopold Tight. Doug now installed as Mavis's boyfriend tagged along as well. Meanwhile the West End musical, The Boyfriend was on tour at Gumption's Coliseum for one week only. In the lead role was Parton's snappy Ethel Patterson Doug knew, but his girlfriend declined go, stamped her petulant foot was

Tales from Planet Gumption

adamant.

Doug settled down for the quiet life with a steady girlfriend. He bought a small modest A30 Austin car from 'Mac's at Ambleside. 'Mac still looked close to death but was pleased to see him. Behind his desk he had pinned all Doug's postcards sent from every port. His aerogrammes neatly preserved inside an old shoebox on his desk. 'Mac's parting shot.

"Go to church son, get married and settle down. Come and see me anytime."

The old man's eyes had misted over as he closed his office door.

But life at No123 was not the best, an impossible place to study and call home, it had not changed a bit. So the Pricket's kindly took the initiative and allocated a space where he could study peacefully at a proper desk. Meanwhile her inside now aged eighteen plus had this great idea they would get married as soon as possible.

In those days it was the forlorn dream of most apprentices and young ladies who worked behind the counter at Woolworths; resided in boxed-in terraced houses seldom seen hot water, panicked in their unlit backyard toilet and tolerated discarded betting slips underfoot. Marry money, preferably to lookalike James Dean or alternatively the girl next door Debbie Reynolds the foremost in their childish dreams. Clamber out of their kitchen sink environment; discard boiler suits or plastic uniforms. Reside in Runners Park Road or just out of town with a garden, a proper lounge where a photo of their little girl in ballet tutu preened. But those who made the effort to impress a local business man's daughter or son often failed when they left and attended a distant College or University. She or he would return from Newcastle with a Solicitor, or a mildewed eyed Fellow she or he had met during ancient History Tutorials, to be only frowned upon by her or his up market parents when they found out her or his father was a Miner; scratched and not a penny to it. The town was full of failed romantics. But what happens when Fred fits in and is taken for what he is? It would be unthinkable and totally unexpected.

The day Doug passed his exams, they all went out for lunch and celebrated. Then as they sat there in the car Mrs. Pricket gave him a Mechanical Engineer's Diary as a present and a record of the times. It was inevitable he had grown fond of Mavis's industrious hard working parents, they were generous and kind, old fashioned but undeniably ambitious. They trusted him and he was of the mind he would never break their trust. Mind you when Rita found some pubic hairs between the spare bedroom's sheets, all hell broke out. Then settled back and was placed on hold in case she found some more. The opportunity to make their daughter pregnant was always there, and he was not keen on Durex. There were other ways to avoid a crisis. Anyhow it was not the way for him, besides he was not the first and said so to implacable Rita inside her own kitchen. Surprisingly, she did not clout him. Instead said simply,

"I know."

Shrugged her shoulders in a huff and walked away. She had approved of Cyril Prince's relationship with her daughter. But to Doug he believed their relationship was convenient for everyone and was fine the way it was, yet softly, softly her parents planned otherwise.

When Doug's results arrived in the mail, he went straight to Personnel and applied for a staff position in one of the Shipyard's Drawing Offices. Plucked up courage and pushed aside the negativity of his Scotland set-to with senior management. Still concerned by the positive response he received when just fresh back from up north and in Dalton Road. When folk, some he did not know pulled him up and shook his hand. He was even stopped by the suspect Head Foreman's joyful nephew. The same man who grabbed him by the shoulders like a long lost brother and shook him to bits. Street wise his Scottish escapade had been approved and endorsed by the masses. Yet as he stood outside Personnel's plain glassed tacky office he was apprehensive and prepared for rejection. He was mistaken and relieved when the stooped shabby blue striped suited hesitant snotty nosed old man returned coughed cleared his throat said clear as a bell.

"Hey-up son, you're booked in with Jack Spratt this afternoon at 2.00pm."

Jack was the Technical Manager of the Railway Sidings Office; seen locally as the outfit which kept Pickersgill's Shipyard financial during before and after WW2. A noted snappy dresser; wore a dark pin striped suit with a rose in his lapel and came with expansive gestures. He knew all about Doug and his 'Teach Your-self Calculus Book', he always carried heavily bookmarked tucked away in the back pocket of his boiler suit. Jack told him he too had started life on a center lathe in the

Michael Stockdale

Shipyard and studied part-time at the local College. It was the result Doug needed at that succinct moment, but slightly iffy at two quid a week less than what he already earned on shifts.

Status wise, he had just stepped up a rung, a Shipyard Staff position in the RSO, the best poorly paid office job in town, but a respectable profession. Fixed up for his entire working life, dictated by annual increases in his pay, yet the girl he courted would soon be headed south as part of her parents' Grand Plan. Her antics preceded by tears and hysterics reenacted every day. Then one sunny Sunday afternoon, Mrs. Pricket and Mavis watched through a kitchen window as the lad helped Albert mow his lawn. Two women, mother and child watched on and wept. Was it tears of joy or plain compassion for the young man who assisted the aged not so very well old man, or because they both knew everyone's time was running out?

It might have been the day before Mavis planned they would run away and get married at Gretna Green. Or when he sold his humble Austin A30 and turned up with a "NOT" approved expensive vintage maroon SS Jaguar Sports car purchased from car enthusiast Curwen Bentley's garage, Mavis hated. Ten miles to the gallon kept inside a rented Abbey Road garage, twenty bob a week, an extravagant acquisition which could keep him broke for years. The Low Hall girl had left a note and packed a suitcase, they would meet at dawn outside the village shop, but Doug did not have the metal and stayed home in bed.

The decision was made and Mavis was enrolled into Anne Hathaway's Ladies College, but why he did not know, or had not quite

Tales from Planet Gumption

worked out. To go all the way to London to check out Fruit Wholesalers in Yellow Pages sounded stupid. Meanwhile he maintained his self-imposed regime at the Pricket's house and Mavis's intermittent visits up from College continued. The lad was always there to meet and pick her up off the last train into Ulverston's lonely heart's Station. He had grown use to what now appeared to be a well-rehearsed frantic dash across the platform to his waiting arms. It now seemed orchestrated and artificial. Doug sensed he had become her ace in the hole in case post Shakespeare did not work out.

Then somewhere along the line she told him Cyril Prince, her former boyfriend had dropped in and that they had driven down to Brighton to watch the sun rise. He might have very well dropped in many times. Cyril was now a University student, studied engineering. Ten to one something special was already lined up for him in the Shipyard. His Dad, Philip Prince was now in charge of the newly created Mechanics Department as well as the Dockyard. It might have been a threat or she had edged her bets, he did not really care, she was with him inside his car, steamed up and stayed an hour.

Now then Doug was not daft or thick but was intensely curious about this southern place called London, the City she said was boring, so overrated he applied for a top job with London Pax and received an offer. But when he showed it to her she tore it up, said forget it. Home again; home again after he picked her up at Ulverston Station but when they arrived at Low Hall it was strangely empty, no one was at home to greet her. It seemed to be a planned event perhaps rehearsed several times the hesitant words

Michael Stockdale

"I've met someone else."

Rendered bluntly, he walked away and left her to it. This courting business had become far too complicated. All this come on tripe about other men put to rest when she arrived next day and knocked on No123's door. On the footpath one packed suitcase, her very first time inside his parent's house. Soon Rita, double Beta her irate mother barged in unannounced; bounded straight through No123's open vestibule and galloped along its long high corridor into its shallow parlor; never once before. Boldly confronted his startled Dad and frowning Mam, her target their lad sat at the table.

"We'll give them one thousand pounds to get started. I've had enough of this."

Then barged straight out again with Mavis in tow and left the vestibule door wide open.

There was silence at the table after they left. Dad's rage stifled Mam in tears. Doug rose and left the table; wandered aimlessly outside. Sought solace on "The Backs" moodily kicked an empty can around the cinder car-park unable to relate to Rita's sudden outburst. There had to be another reason. Disconcerted, that she and Albert believed that they could buy anything. Balanced the books tried for an ace in the hole.

"We'll call you and raise you one thousand quid. We'll take that lad there on the shelf, boxed, bound and filed."

Tales from Planet Gumption

It was now that time of year when Gumption's young men and women of a certain age were pressured by families to get married and legs parted. Encouraged to pause outside jewelers shops, try on rings. Start buying blankets, new towels any old thing to be hoarded; prepare the way, stored in a special box kept in the best room. Privacy encouraged time and again always the best room. Outside in the parlor an entire family grouped waited.

"Hey-up they're engaged."

Gumption's, annual plague of marriages of convenience had commenced.

"He's a good lad saved forty quid," or "Don't mess about if she's pregnant."

It never happened. It was late summer when Doug crashed his SS Jaguar near Hindpool's Garden of Eden and blamed the accident on some very bad news, the axing of the Shipyard's Rail Sidings Office where he worked and not his argument with Mavis. He had thought she would be pleased to hear he had reapplied to London Pax to navigate away from subsequent Gumption dole queues. No such luck, instead of joyful squeals she had grabbed the hand-made steering wheel of his expensive vintage car and rammed it into Hindpool's exclusive Church of England Primary School slate wall. The school's head teacher a languid Miss Jean Mac Taggart who favored kilts, Scottish thrift charged Mavis 10p to phone her Dad from her office.

Michael Stockdale

Twenty minutes later Albert arrived in panic mode and offered to drive Doug home too. But Mavis would have none it said they were finished. Her Dad resigned, scratched his head, his expression classic cocker spaniel threw in his two bob's worth.

"Hey-up Douglas, I've contacted Curwen's Tow Trucks to pick it up."

Just as the local Ribble bus came into sight.

"Thanks a lot. I'll see you later," yelled Doug.

Signaled the driver and stopped the bus. Climbed aboard and claimed his inherent right, that of an independent born optimist.

Time passed and when Doug researched the going market for vintage 1936 SS Jaguar sports cars, he discovered that the Earl of Frizington the original owner had had it built to his own specifications. This single piece of information immediately attracted a much higher value than what he had paid, three hundred pounds and his late model A30 Austin, now valued at well over six thousand sterling. It occurred to him he should capitalize on his good fortune and perhaps also change his image. He placed an advertisement 'as is' in Motor Magazine. The Jaguar sold within weeks to Relic's Rare Car Museum. Not only did Doug receive all his hard earned cash back, he made five thousand quid profit. Then shrewdly decided to go down market and buy an unsellable fuel hungry Armstrong (Bentley grill) Bonneville modified coupe with dropped suspension for seven hundred quid. Rear flat tray, extended cabin with four ox-hide seats, brand-new imported V8 USA engine; four spot lights, two stainless steel exhausts ex-Premier Motor Dealers and listened to an old familiar Keno rumble.

Drove and parked it behind 123 Lord Street and revved the engine. His old Dad galloped soon outside in a state of flux because it dislodged 123's parlor windows. Tugged at the Armstrong's cabin driver's side handle and cried out.

"What the hell is this you've gone and done our Douglas?"

"Hi-yah Dad, listen to this," grinned his response.

Laughed and pressed the Armstrong's horn several times, the wail from its blunt exterior reminiscent of the Shipyard's ex-WW2 hooter. Now flush with funds and new state carriage he changed direction. Said yes to London Pax Personnel's detailed offer, sent an acceptance telegram via Rawlinson Street Post Office and was on his way.

The news was out, Doug's confidante The Pie Lady a little envious swallowed a lump in her throat when early morning the man from 123 loaded up his mean machine drove off and headed east alone. Turned right at Leven's Bridge and left the womb. His tempered EN3A steel umbilical cord not entirely severed. Gumption's microcosm of life in short hand; failed romantics intertwined, another corner stone of life. Idle thoughts simply jettisoned past the beast's spaceship styled, brushed stainless steel dashboard. 'Jezebel's' interior large enough for him to

Michael Stockdale

sleep in any bye-way in the land. Above his head a see-through tinted sliding window, fully air-conditioned, world-wide coverage on his international radio. Doug's calling card did few miles to the gallon, his fat wallet not in the slightest interested; murmured.

"Take me south, you modified Armstrong (Bentley grill) dropped suspension. Rear flat tray, eighteen inch wheels all weather tires, extended cabin tinted glass with four ox-hide seats, brand-new imported V8 engine; four spot lights. Guided missile stainless steel bass baritone exhausts. What better place to head for than to London in the sixties?"

Twelve hours later the Policeman's torch awoke two 'lovers' fast asleep inside the Armstrong parked on London's Hampstead Heath.

"Hello, hello what have we here? You can't kip there," voiced a jolly, laughing London Bobbie, notebook out, grinned licked his pencil.

"You're nicked; names and addresses please," pointed his pencil at the girl, "We'll start with you."

The couple squirmed as he jotted down their details then when satisfied all was well said "Clear off". Douglas started up the Armstrong's engine easy on the pedal, looked at Mavis's face. She was smiling.

Faraway and much later, upstairs in Low Hall Albert took the call,

"What's this?" he cried, chin wobbling woolen dressing gown all askew, his half lit fag made him gasp for air. He groaned out aloud switched on all bedroom lights then mumbled his long telephone conversation with a London Bobby to half asleep her in curlers Rita.

"Wake up lovey, that little bugger Douglas was two hours ago, according to the Police, found asleep with our Mavis on Hampstead Heath in that bloody Tradesman's vehicle of his. What's going on, I've had enough of this malarkey?"

Around one in the morning our errant couple found a small Hotel and slept the night in a single bed. Morning glory no real drama, his female environmentalist, pissed into the wash basin like a professional. Exponentially groomed grinned at the mirror after a fried up breakfast then via Tube back to Hathaway's College, en suite toilets and separate bathrooms. Doug to his Wood Green digs then back to work at London Pax.

Magistrates can be useful people. Soon one similar self-important earnest friend and wife shared Madeira cake and coffee with their closest friends, prominent Gumption Hairdressers' at their dining table. Sharp faced Sydney Leopold Tight the Magistrate summed up.

"Well, dearie me I don't know. Overall he seemed a decent lad to me. I suppose Rita could go down to London?"

Placed both hands on the table fingers pointed, as if in prayer nodded to purple faced, nudged Rita of the baggy eyes and unrepentant liver.

"Why not stay awhile and talk with her? If all else fails, you may require some professional advice to sort it out."

Three cigarette's later, Albert miles away somewhere else, shot bolt upright in his chair slightly breathless.

"Aye he's a good lad that one, I liked his metal. He studied hard and lived like a bloody Monk. It's our Mavis that bothers me." Paused, looked at Rita and nodded his head.

"You know she's wilder than him at times. Maybe we should let it settle."

Rita's face went black, glared rose quietly to her feet and faced the men.

"I'm fed up with all this too. I'll pack my suitcase straight away. I could be in London by tonight."

Doug's Wood Green boarding house accommodation was listed and recommended by London Pax. He had moved in and soon received an edict from Mavis, their Hampstead Heath liaison was now common knowledge; please stay away until further notice. Then as if on cue his boarding house was raided by the police. Turned out it was a 24/7 Brothel. In need of cheer, he fled to the only Pub he knew The Spaniard's buried at the top end of Hampstead. The Pub was deserted. Business was flat except for two expensive looking women who drank whiskey alone and ignored anyone who may have been interested. "Hmmm," thought to be too up market for the Gumption man. Left his half-finished light ale aware nothing was doing and called it a day.

Tales from Planet Gumption

Outside, the Pub's austere car park was almost empty. The smell, the rancid combination of shit, piss and beer suggested it was well patronized or badly managed. The Spaniard's car-park's sole floodlight was false economy, its beam muffled and distorted by clouds of insects. Unchallenged to date, since the Armstrong's exhaust pipes had been adjusted, it rested unattended at the rear. The suburb's air handicapped by a vapid silence, still but humid. Broken suddenly by high pitched piercing screams which Doug assumed to come from a small sedan, positioned straight ahead the only other car visible partially hidden in the shadows. Sharp silhouettes of two short thickset men in suits who held both doors wide open. Inside two panic stricken women struggled to disbar them. Doug started up his Armstrong's V8 engine. Ominous deep sonorous growls emitted from its two bass baritone exhausts. Instant daylight, when he switched on all lights and bedlam when he pressed his WW2 siren horn just a fraction. Doug yelled out and ran towards the action. Felt the rush of adrenaline. Crazed paved when he reached them. Both men lurched off swallowed by the darkness; one woman's dress was torn. The other sobbed, was hysterical; Doug caught as she stumbled and nearly fell.

He recognized the women from inside the Pub. They took some time to quiet down. Both lit cigarettes and reflected; they had nearly made London's papers. It was obvious Doug was from up north but the presence of the Armstrong projected a more or less apt but misleading image. They spoke in twang a twang voices said he deserved a small reward and he settled for a coffee, but as they lived in Kensington he did not know the way. They suggested he should follow them and they drove off to the City and parked outside Kensington Mews, where one apparently lived inside a swish three bedroomed flat. They might have been two up market prostitutes on the game. Doug did not know who they were and did not really care.

Not much more than a few weeks in from up north, the Gumption man was about to find out why Mavis and her parents did not want him there. They had watched it all on Thames ITV seated in Low Hall's lounge, smiled and nodded knowingly to each other then gently passed around assorted sandwiches. Still in context but miles away Doug had just met two gorgeous London women without the need of long newsy letters ex NW3 on a platter who served him Irish coffee in a dainty cup. Close to midnight her friend left and they chatted seated on separate chairs. Sensed their worlds were miles apart. Her auburn styled twang a twang hair said her name was Rachel, modeled bridal gowns in the City and showed him photographs. Presented him with a unique first edition and they arranged to meet in Hampstead on Saturday, the following day.

They met again outside Belsize Tube Station. She looked chic; straight out of Vogue or as seen in one of Rita Pricket's fashion magazines stacked inside her Fine Lace Hair Salon. Wore a red beret, silk see through blouse, red mini-skirt, white Italian knee high boots, perfect teeth. Supremely confident, she placed one affectionate arm around his shoulders and guided him to a small shop window. Top left hand corner, 'Flats to Rent' listed via hand written postcards. She quickly found one she recommended, 'Furnished two-bed flat with study ten guineas per week.' Or half his London Pax wages; Rachel thought a bargain.

Tales from Planet Gumption

They made the call and were met by two gay middle aged men who drove an old Rolls Royce. To the rear of London's Old money Doug parked the ubiquitous non-groveling assertive no apologies Armstrong. Two now nervous gay men agreeably led them in, primarily impressed by Rachel's twang a twang. Both ex-theatricals made extra money by refurbishing and renting out flats on behalf of two old ladies who owned the building. Old Biddies they would never meet because they lived down in the basement. Doug's flat for rent was magnificent and spacious, high ornate ceilings; crystal chandeliers and included an ornamental balcony hidden behind four white French doors. Each door reflected vivid colors from a small garden outside. Genuine antique furniture; marshaled by two fine Italian Marble fireplaces; a tiny but well equipped kitchen. A sudden nudge from Rachel, he would need to buy a casserole. Doug showed the common touch flashed a fat roll of fivers and paid his deposit. This action stopped the gay boys in their tracks and he moved from Wood Green that very day and carefully placed Rachel's photo on the mantel piece. Then lay on his King size bed and thought of dear Agnes; two inch finger nails painted orange, tattooed shoulders and fell asleep contented.

The Chief Designer at London Pax took the call and waved to newly appointed Designer Warrington/Boiler Division up to his neck with diagrams, calculations and assorted calorific values.

"Some broad called Mavis."

Doug had not seen much or thought of Mavis since their Hampstead

Michael Stockdale

Heath liaison and took the call.

"Not now," but gave her his new address and contact number. Then wondered why he had bothered. She had been placed on the back burner somewhere between the Spaniard's Pub and Kensington Mews.

Days later Mavis buzzed Doug's intercom and climbed the wooden stairs to his first floor Palace. Entered minus riding crop out of nowhere said "What-oh," then strolled around as if she owned it; him too, lock stock and barrel but balked at a kiss. Railed at the photograph of Rachel, Lady Rachel Edwina Eleanor Cooper-Spottiswood down from the Cotswold's, there on his mantel piece and quickly threw it out of his open French doors. Declared war; stomped out and past two other tenants. Both bespectacled American University lecturers on one year's Sabbatical. Proclaimed to all and sundry,

"I'm now officially Douglas Warrington's ex-girlfriend."

Doug had no idea he was famous or that she was three months pregnant.

But her mother Rita did, she had done her sums and eliminated him as prime suspect. Her Dad Albert, the betting man, had immediately labeled lithe Cyril Prince the odds on favorite. But when approached Top Gun Philip Prince was not concerned either way,

"She'd seemed an awkward filly from the beginning."

Cyril Prince according to Agnes, who now and again dropped Doug a

Tales from Planet Gumption

line wrote, 'Cyril no longer attends Gospel Hall.'

The sun always seemed to smile in London. London's weather did not disappoint compared to the usual Gumption blast from across the Irish Sea. It was never bitter or freezing cold. London's weather was to Doug's advantage as a northerner, he rarely wore an overcoat or his ex-Marine string vest in public. Rachel's numerically assessed romantic period now equated to wedding bells and marriage in the City. She had tired of dragging him outside jewelry shop windows in search of an engagement ring to sedate her impatient Dowager mother. She had vaguely mentioned she was 27 when they first met, but her mother in a moment of drama one weekend at their Cotswold spread, let it drop she was perhaps closer to 37 and had missed the boat. Weakened, and succumbed by her volatile outbursts, all because he had not risen to her expectations.

"She'd never met his parents, why not?"

Complained when he disappeared and did not invite her to distant Gumption, wherever the hell that was, on public holidays. Doug now regarded by Rachel's parents as her surreptitious lover and a total waste of time. The very last thing they and Rachel expected was the sudden invitation to meet Doug's parents.

Doug had never mentioned Chantilly since confronted by an article salvaged from Gumption's NWEM. Then out of the blue and just before his planned visit to Gumption with Rachel, he received another unexpected telephone call at London Pax. "Some broad," called out his boss deep in thought and transferred the call to Doug's extension. Doug once alerted grabbed pencil and paper; startled by his caller's voice gasped.

"Whoa, is that Chantilly? Where the hell are you?"

Stunned his Yukon past had finally tracked him down. She still possessed the same old tinker bell persuasive voice.

"Hello honey. We're just passing through and ah thought I'd give yah a call. If yah aren't too busy why not join us for dinner tonight? I've something to show yah honey. Say 7.00 pm at Flanagan's in Baker Street."

Doug said nothing, his situation had suddenly changed. For a moment his caller thought he had hung up. Doug now out of bottom gear responded.

"Wow! I don't believe it. How are you Pet and where are you?"

Played for time and did a reality check. He had nothing to lose; snapped to it with more enthusiasm.

"*That* would be really champion by me. How long is it now? I'm looking forward to it. See you at seven then."

Accidently hung up: Stood limp in silence by the phone. He had no idea what to expect but was extremely curious. His nagging question, where in hell had she got his work number?

Tales from Planet Gumption

Flanagan's fish delicacies were popular in the City but being Tuesday it was quiet when he entered. Stood and waited at reception next to the Cashier's celebrated sedan chair. Recognized an old familiar voice from inside the restaurant, "Over here honey," guided him to a secluded table and a much slimmer, exquisitely dressed elated Chantilly in company. Seated opposite, a small child and almost whispered.

"Say, hello to your father Victor."

Strapped for words Douglas sat down. Looked closely at the lad and grinned, nudged the child gently on the shoulder.

"Hello son, you've got to be kidding?"

Chantilly laughed and caressed the child.

"No doubt about it honey, and that's why I'm here."

She puckered up for a kiss. Doug blushed, kissed her gently and felt a shiver go up his spine. Chantilly stroked his face and smiled.

"Ah knew yah climbed back up that stockpile honey. Ah could see yah all the time. That's why the ceremony went ahead, then stalled and made it world-wide on television."

'Christ Almighty,' thought Doug, weak at the knees shook his head from side to side. He knew shit knew nothing knew fuck all.

Michael Stockdale

"Anyhow honey," Chantilly retained her posture, idly flicked through the Menu then looked deeply into Doug's eyes.

"I'm here to offer yah a proposition and I don't intend to twist your arm."

She then leaned back, waved a royal hand and attracted the immediate attention of two instant waiters' ordered champagne. It arrived with speed and a flourish, she raised her glass smiled knowingly, knew her man; glowed.

"Here's to us and to something different."

Douglas dazed by her frank admission, the little boy sat on his knees looked just like him. He was a Dad! It seemed both feasible yet ridiculous.

Chantilly meanwhile again scanned the menu, ordered two seafood platters, one small plate of finely chopped calamari for little Victor and probed Doug's memory.

"Didn't yah once sell cars for Mac's of Ambleside?"

"Aye, of course I did. By gum, swapped forty quid per week for a measly forty quid foreign bound a month. I liked Mac a lot, he really trusted me. But I heard he'd passed away."

Tales from Planet Gumption

"Listen up honey." Savaged her lobster waved her fork,

"Mac was my father's eldest brother and Mac left him the business. Yah even rated an honorable mention in dispatches, right?"

"When I think of it, Mac did mutter something about no real heirs for his business. Aye: About the time I told him I'd opted to join the Merchant Navy instead of National Service. But there again what's all this got to do we' me?"

"Well, Mac's family also owned land and sand mining options still valid today, on Gumption's Walney Island thought to be useless for generations. Dad had it assayed last year and discovered it contained rare minerals worth a fortune."

"Hang on; I've no experience in mining except for Keno Hill."

"It doesn't matter honey," laughed rubbed her hips. "Yah made a big impression at Keno. Call it instinct. Remember your big plan to do something about your qualifications? My Dad started life in a trade and would've financed your engineering studies anyhow. You weren't to know. I figured if yah did you'd have cleared off anyway. We've watched your progress from afar. Now you're technically qualified in marine and mechanical engineering, impressively financed by yourself as planned. This I know because Dad hired Pinkerton's without me knowing, tracked yah down and checked yah out."

"Bloody hell, you'll know about the other women too?"

Michael Stockdale

Chantilly ignored the question and responded lightly.

"Dad wants you as CEO of Lode Consolidated Mineral Sands, to act on behalf of one of its major shareholders, meaning our son Victor, that child on your knee. You'll receive a no strings attached handsome package. Here's our offer in detail, in my capacity as Courier," teased puckered lips and thrust a fat envelope across the table.

"Say tonight at 'Ridges then when business calls between Tarn Manor and Castle Crag Lake Windermere."

It seemed like only yesterday when Doug joined London Pax and now he was leaving. His middle order position involved calculations based on formulae supplied by company manuals and applied to hi-tech gas fired boilers. It was not unusual for someone who relied mainly on company manuals, sometimes to intuitively become more than a specialist. In a way Pax had groomed Doug to become more of a lateral thinker, particularly at monthly Value Analysis meetings. Here, four or five designers would sit around a table armed with a Referee. His or her role was to eliminate digression and to maintain focus entirely on the specific item or subject to hand.

But today he was back in Gumption for two or three days and walked the walk down Dalton Road with up market twang a twang Rachel. Gumption's main street packed with ex-Army & Navy boiler suits nudged each other yelled out

Tales from Planet Gumption

"Hey-up, Doug. Who's the chick?"

Stood outside Kelly's Music Shop crowded entrance a local celebrity. Doug hand in hand with Rachel, an active member of the Committee of One Hundred and ardent Ban the Bomb activist. Articulate, well-educated, refined and beautiful; to his mind at a different time she might have fitted in.

Rachel had been amazed when Doug said to his father all fired up,

"Smarten up and get your bloody hair cut Dad."

Then, appeased Dad's reaction with the offer of two new suits from Levy's Tailors which left him speechless. He was much the same with Mam; dropped her off at the best dress shop in town with orders to go mad and buy up big. But when he called in additional staff to scrub and polish 123 from top to bottom nobody said a word.

On their last day Doug and Rachel bumped into Mavis with her rheumatoid mother and designer pram in Gumption's market. Both mother and daughter backed off with nowhere to hide and never expected a friendly greeting and kiss. Rachel shared cigarettes with Doug's Church Street Grandmother as Doug monitored respectable solicitor Alf Parsons draw up documents for Doug's purchase of her Church Street twenty roomed house: Witnessed by E. Ball Architects who would submit plans to convert into six refurbished flats. Provide a comfortable home and assured income for his one tooth beloved Grandmother and her astute investor.

Michael Stockdale

Mam in tears Dad stiff as a ramrod, proud as Punch stood at the rear of 123 and waved them off, cried.

"See you at Xmas son. She's a lovely girl."

Doug pointed the Armstrong towards Town Hall, passed Gumption Library then drove up Abbey Road. No one spoke until they turned right at Leven's Bridge. Rachel slept until the outskirts of London and they arrived at Kensington Mews around dusk. Settled down and celebrated their return to London with one or two glasses of Scotch before dinner; French Casserole and red wine.

Obsessed with inequality, socialist aristocrat Rachel had always craved for a working class heritage and was convinced her vindication had arrived in the arms of her adorable scrubber Doug. Mummy and Daddy just did not seem to care but aside thought it would be really nice, if she stopped demonstrating and being arrested and finally produced a baby.

But right then Doug had other ideas. Rose up from the table, grabbed his jacket scratched his chin mumbled

"Well, I'll be off then, I'm leaving."

It was the very last thing Rachel expected.

"WHAT? LEAVING?"

Tales from Planet Gumption

She could not believe his affront and leapt bodily off her mahogany Gianni antique settee, nails on the ready. Doug frozen momentarily by her unbridled fury, walked tentatively towards her and attempted to soothe her; stroked both shoulders garnered courage whispered.

"Listen up luv, it's all to do with business and a proposition I need to think about. You've met my parents and now you know which side of the fence I sit. C'mon let's face it, my thoughts on marriage have never changed. You are too good for me, and besides I'm not ready for marriage. I've got things to do."

"DO? Marry you? You ass hole,"

Rachel shrugged him off and rose to her feet screamed, picked up her favorite Aunt's Venetian vase and threw it as he dived for cover.

"You used me you conniving piece of shit. Yes, used me along with all the others."

Stamped both feet, found another missile, her prized Art deco radio and threw it at his head. Drew blood, Doug staggered against one wall; both arms extended protested.

"Steady lass, relax please cool down."

Engulfed with rage Rachel ran towards him clutched a bronze statue of Eros that smashed against his outstretched arms. One arm fractured hung loose by his side. Rachel was not finished, raised her tiny fists and pummeled his unprotected face sobbed.

"Get the fuck out of my life. Fuck off now or I'll call the police."

Doug in shocking pain limped towards the open door unsure where he was. Turned and said softly,

"That's it then? We're finished?"

His question answered by another missile, an iron antique kettle. Knocked off balance, he stumbled and fell down several stairs, skidded down flat on his back into her rain soaked courtyard. Limped towards the Armstrong said weakly, "Hello Son," struggled with its door's handle, climbed inside and grabbed his overnight bag.

Found a shirt and held it with his teeth, with one hand ripped it into strips and pandered to his injured arm. Dug out Rachel's stainless steel flask of tea, soaked a rag and washed his face. Smiled grimly, recognized the image in the windscreen and with irony hummed Eddie Arnold's classic "The Tennessee Stud." Pressed the Armstrong's starter button and slowly drove away.

Through and out of London, he drove all night occupied about his future. He had deliberately been vague in detail to Rachel about his Ambleside asset (Mac's garage and seven acres to be signed over to him as a sweetener: Pending his acceptance of Chantilly's offer). One long term plan was to develop the seven acres into a kind of satellite up market retirement village but he had hedged at first on his relationship with Lode Holdings. But once he had agreed to Chantilly's offer to represent young Victor's interests, unknown to him Lode deposited one hundred and fifty thousand pounds tax paid into his Barclay's Bank account.

As for Rachel he had no idea how old she was, often her hair roots showed up grey. She drank scotch because she could afford to. Enjoyed a dram or two, smoked cigarettes, as if the tide was coming in. But when it was his shout at the pub she always drank brown ale. She was a thoughtful yet independent woman with fading parents who, when in London stayed in a distant cousin's Well Walk, Hampstead apartment. In the old days when they came to town Doug was always invited to lunch. Played cards all afternoon, or chatted but any talk of marriage was taboo. Doug's collection of 'friends' were often exactly that, people he met who were good company or just someone he sympathized with, helped or protected. But his recent no holds barred fight with Rachel unsettled him. Maybe she had needed 'a bit of rough' to turn her on or had lost her marbles once too many times? She was terrified her Old Woman would find out she had met her man inside a Pub car-park. She might have killed him. It did not matter Doug was on a mission. These latter day vagaries fused his thoughts before he fell asleep in a Lindale bye way.

Mavis Pricket inside her school uniform had once cornered Doug amongst the hay while her thin Dad mowed their lawn. Her beautiful baby was not his but it was the one she had always wanted. Happy Grandparents Albert and Rita now semi-retired; sold Low Hall and moved to Windermere. The two of them had gone all casual and passed

Michael Stockdale

the day as owners/part-time managers of "Monsieur Short Cuts" in Bowness. Doug's Church Street development had been approved in principle and would ensure his Church Street Grandmother passed away in sheer luxury. It's only Penthouse would be accessed by private lift, the developed six flats would be managed by fast Cavendish Eddy now a licensed Bookie would occupy its ground floor. Doug's 1959 (Bentley grill) V8 engine Armstrong would be garaged in mothballs in Church Street's proposed underground private car-park.

Before his pending trip overseas Doug had 'retired' Personal Assistant pregnant again Agnes Ripley. Two inch finger nails painted purple tattooed shoulders and now left thigh: Unmarried mother of two with a generous stipend. Doug meanwhile tried to spend more time at Lode's Tarn Manor and fathom out how to utilize its state of the art, packaged IBM communications system. It was heavy going but with the guidance from three skilled key USA technicians provided by Lode's parent company, the data produced suggested Operation X had potential. Computer Aided Drafting was in its infancy and Doug stuck to conventionally prepared engineering drawings. He studied Plant Layouts/Flow Charts and as he progressed was staggered by their increased estimated sand mining costs. Initially, the amount of funds required had appeared reasonable but now seemed prohibitive. But necessary in the development and ultimate submission of what was seen as an environmental sensitive operation. The latest technology of sand separation equipment appeared to be based thousands of miles away. One large active plant owned by a South African mining company based in Johannesburg, was Zircon Rutile south of Brisbane and another called Miserable Deposits on the Gold Coast, both thrived in Australia.

Tales from Planet Gumption

One more trip to Gumption to say cheerio to his parents and Joe. Then perhaps a solitary walk down memory lane, catch up with his Church Street Grandmother and take a final stroll down Dalton Road. Maybe he would call in to see how E. Ball Architects had progressed, then coffee at Brucciani's. Understandably, apprehensive since NWEM published a negative sand-mining article and pointed the finger at Lode's preliminary activities on Walney Island. The news was out. Beware the environmentalists, particularly Rachel the activist who would latch on to anything controversial. Inside his overcoat pocket he carried his Qantas flight tickets and Chantilly's last telegram, "Go get them honey, love and kisses "C and V."

Via Qantas

Agnes Ripley was never glib, clipped her nails sliced her locks colored blonde and always said it as it was: Posed outside **'Ripper Health Foods,'** her most recent acquisition. Reflected through its main window stood Gumption's largest Shipyard crane painted pink, laced with fresh daffodils. Photographed madly by NWEM held hands with eldest son Norman and toddler Stanley, cried her eyes out and wept with joy. The sign out front said, **'THE BEST SASSAPARILLA IN TOWN,'** her Mam and Dad Norman her very first customers.

Somewhere else and further south, Fleet Street pandered to assertive academic Germaine Greer interviewed by Frost criticized British Media. Further north and not at all sanctimonious, Gerry and the Pacemakers sang 'Ferry across the Mersey.' Played over Lakeland's Laundry intercom, echoed British sentiments and nobody smoked a pipe except its floor manager and PM Harold Wilson. Northern England's Telephone exchanges switched on off. Rule Britannia please stand; only on Saturdays at the Proms as early snow blanketed Heathrow Airport.

The unannounced late arrival of ex-car salesman, high seas mariner Douglas V for Victor Warrington, climbed aboard two steps at a time Qantas Flight 236. Grinned boldly flirted with her in curlers chortled,

"Hey-up luv, slept in again eh?"

Squatter's daughter Flight Attendant April Showers chewed tobacco not amused, preferred mature hirsute Aryan blonds, suffered from a ding-bat hang-over. Disliked corny gags intensely and very nearly thumped him. Aged 39 at six foot three submitted when she read his Qantas boarding pass said first class.

Doug wore a smooth expensive camel coat, three piece fine merino wool grey suit but underneath his blue fine Italian cotton shirt relied on his two quid ex-Army and Navy Stores string vest. His black curly hair cropped, both hands on hips flashed his teeth amazed and gawped deep inside Flight Q236's Aladdin's Cave. Above and along both sides stretched layer after layer of aborigine murals delicately balanced by muted lighting. Mysterious shapes and patterns painted throughout the Jumbo's egg-shaped interior substantiated by melodic indigenous chants from the Antipodes.

Tales from Planet Gumption

Primeval echoes from the past mesmerized Doug. He fell asleep as the plane ascended. Memories of his first sighting of Lake Maracaibo's steamy muddy waters aboard Fischer's Tanker MV Marigold came floating back. The vessel's destination crowded by matted mangroves and Venezuela's impenetrable jungle. No mail since he left home. Three months had passed at sea and now on 'movements,' watch's reduced to four hours on and four hours off as the vessel crawled across the vast and treacherous Maracaibo. Finally the bridge signaled stop engines, not much breeze on deck, hot as hell below; no ventilated air and those below drank weak sweet tea by the gallon from an alumina jug. Swallowed hard fat circular salt tablets that scratched their gullets. Up top, the ship berthed alongside a large pontoon then secured, surrounded by the Maracaibo's swirling murky waters.

The Tanker's shabby well-worn prow had by now faced the effigy of Conrad's 'Heart of Darkness' dense jungle many times: One hundred degrees on deck, sheer hell down below and from the ship's loud speakers' episode 3,567, 000 of BBC Overseas Mrs. Dale's Diary, always in crisis. 'The price of English bread to rise again,' direct from London. The reality when three armed soldiers noiselessly climbed aboard, highlighted by vivid lightning bolts. Enlisted men but looked like brigands provided by the Government, wore bright red bandanas. Carried large ammunition belts slung around their shoulders and wielded blunt automatic weapons. Each soldier positioned in three strategic locations to belay unwelcome boarders, one at mid-ships, one forward and aft.

Once the Tanker was loaded with oil, all soldiers were ferried ashore and the ship upped anchor; turned slowly on 'movements' and hours later tracked past Curacao into a strange sudden acute calm or heavy silence. The noise from its diesel magnified as the horizon vanished under a blanket of aggressive sheer black clouds. Within minutes a mighty cyclonic wind tore across the vessel. All hands paralyzed without warning, unable to gauge or avoid the surging mountainous swell which followed. The entire ship enveloped by an instant violent storm. Any object not secured, including men devoured instantly by the maelstrom. Two men swept overboard considered lost. The Skipper's final order was to let the vessel run with the sea. The matchbox ship bottomed and shuddered. 10000 tons pitched bodily by more broadsides. The virulent sea swamped the main cat walk and inundated cabins. From the bridge, the ship's arterial catwalk seemed perennially submerged. Swamped, the main deck cleared and swollen each time she rolled. All around frantic SOS's filtered in from stricken ships some already doomed, visibility down to the wire, the Marigold's fog siren dead and out of action.

Fools and mad men sent one man aft, another up forward. Each one carried an empty oil drum and futile hammer. Both wisely climbed inboard for safety. Rum spilled from the fear stricken Skipper's bottle. Watches jeopardized. He ordered up a long heavy rope to gain access to the Engine room via the mid-ship's catwalk. The definite risk of being washed overboard delayed all major decisions.

Doug's watch commenced at midnight until four in the morning. He would be the first to take the rope close to 12.00 p.m. Convinced this would be as close to suicide he would get and took his time. He was in no rush to die and conversed with his inner self.

Tales from Planet Gumption

"If there was a God, God would be a pal and watch his back."

More on his knees than feet he crawled along the narrow catwalk. His shadowy figure buffeted as she rolled. Doug continued slowly aft as best he could. But found the engine room door jammed and panicked. For one brief second lost bodily contact with both the deck and door handle convinced he was a goner. One short mad hysterical laugh was all he could muster. Then suddenly underfoot he felt the deck and with both hands grasped the Engine Room door handle. Once inside he scrambled down the series of step ladders down to the ship's bowels then made his way to the Engine Room desk and main controls. It was eerie to be alone inside the silent Engine room. The main engine captured in motion. The ship listed. Packs of cigarettes and the vital Engine-room log scattered underfoot. There was no communication from the Bridge. Frantic and inexperienced he went off to search for the watch's boiler man determined to start the engine. But found him drunk and incoherent aft, sprawled on his bunk in the crew's quarters.

Doug elected to trek back up forward to relay his findings. The youngest officer on board with little or no authority entered the Chief Engineer's cabin and found everyone incapably drunk. To his mind they had given up and deserted the ship. Some offered booze and everyone ignored his pleas. Instead, they stood as one and toasted Spud Murphy the Ship's crazed Radio Officer barricaded in his cabin. Doug left them to it. Off aft to find a sober boiler man. Grabbed 'Gregorio the Wop' and managed to start the compressor. Soon joined reluctantly by two other engineers and between them fired the engine. The storm eased half an hour later, but up top madness still prevailed. The overbearing facts; two married men had been lost and that many ships had gone down in the blow. Meanwhile their intoxicated Skipper was unable to unlock the Radio Officer's cabin door and ordered one of the Mates to smash it down with a fire axe. Inside the Irishman sprawled on his bunk terrified, only the whites of his eyes visible. They imprisoned in the only prison on board, a canvas strait jacket.

Blue skies above, up forward at long last and in the distance the English coastline. It happened when the Pilot came on board and all mail was delivered. The Gumption man did not expect any mail. Yet on his cabin desk he found a pile of mail, from pals or girl-friends. They had written all the time but their letters lacked 'sufficient' postage stamps. The company had declined to absorb these costs or debit him, but why he would never know. He now had no respect for the Company, Captain and the subsequent dereliction of duty by his superiors. To his mind they had deserted the ship and placed everyone's life at risk. Ten seconds and within sight of the cliffs of Dover, Doug advised the Skipper this would be his last trip.

The Old Man beset with varicose blue veins contacted their City Superintendent via ship's phone who tackily declined Doug's resignation with the threat.

"You'll be fucking blacklisted for life."

Well, it was too late now Doug had already packed his gear and lined up in the Officer's Mess to sign off. By the length of the queue, most or all of the ship's crew were leaving too. The Skipper's already maligned reputation now marred by superstition. Their indolent master doomed to write a negative report. In the background two burly lover boys postulated hands on hips, stood to one side and leered. When Doug signed off at Albert Dock the Skipper's eyes were blank and unseeing. One short stroll down the gang plank, he was gone.

Flight Attendant April Showers leaned over Doug's limp figure and wondered if she should wake him. His garbled fucking and blinding had raised her fears albeit minor. Her father could out swear a platoon of Anzacs any day. She toyed again with waking Doug until she caught his almost childlike self-depreciating grin, heard him murmur "Aye," in agreement and gave the idea of waking him away, well at least for another half hour.

Cunard's unexpected 'one liner' telex had arrived direct from their Liverpool office which more or less said come on down position vacant. Doug had pushed for a next day appointment, caught the first train south and walked to Cunard's Liver Buildings. They were impressive, of another generation and sharply defined by the broad expanse of the river Mersey. Once inside he was met by a mélange of boot polish, wood stain, Navy Plug pipe tobacco and salt, large heavy doors suspended from greased once a month huge brass hinges. Erect and obliging old men in patched creased suits leisurely gave directions. He was expected; knocked. From within a voice rasped the affected "Come."

At a glance the Superintendent's office possessed an extraordinary high ceiling with ornate cornices. Large windows, teak ledges used as

Michael Stockdale

bookcases. Up above an old fashioned brass fan and down below perhaps a memento from an Imperial past a faded Indian mat. On the facing wall a large black and white photograph of the RMS Queen Mary its decks crowded with returning WW2 American servicemen. The Statue of Liberty, in the background Manhattan's Skyline the mighty ship had outraced the U-Boats on her way to New York's Harbor. So many stories suspended high and pitched directly above the man who had said come.

Doug stood and waited patiently until offered a chair. Gazed around the office and tactfully avoided the Indian mat in front of the man's paneled desk. Studied his interviewer's non-threatening profile; Archie Middleton appeared slight, short of hair balding middle aged and wore a modest frayed green tweed jacket, elbows economically patched with thin red leather. One flapped when he finally nodded.

"Please take a chair and let's have a look at your Discharge Book."

Doug placed the hard backed reference article on the desk. Utter silence reigned as the Superintendent's fingers fiddled uncomfortably around D.V. Warrington's Mercantile Marine Discharge Book. He closed abruptly then picked about its hard dark blue corners as if he had missed a page frowned, raised and lowered his unclipped black bushy eyebrows twice, said "Um." Produced a pair of thin metal framed spectacles from a pocket, retrieved a handkerchief, slowly and methodically cleaned their lens. Placed them on his impish nose, stretched backwards in his flexible chair and pursed his lips. Almost whispered and confided.

"You've been blacklisted by your previous employer son. What have

Tales from Planet Gumption

you got to say about that?"

Doug was circumspect with his reply, shrugged and kept it simple with no excuses.

"We were hit by a violent storm outside of Curacao and lost engines. The officers thought they were goners, got drunk and abandoned the ship. All I did was to resign when we berthed at Albert Dock."

"Resign?"

"Aye, said Doug, "And I gave them plenty of time to find a replacement."

The Superintendent hesitant, chewed invisible cud and remained expressionless aware the lad was obviously young and green. Gazed at the wall behind the youngster and voyaged back in time. To another terrifying storm that occurred so very long ago around the Cape. When badly maintained life boat davits jammed and grown men panicked when he too was young and new to the sea. Shook his head from side to side exhaled gone again, moodily in another time and place. Suddenly snapped to it, bunched two long fingered powerful hands and slowly leant forward with a suspiciously knowing grin.

"Let's see now. Why not start today? They need someone here in Liverpool to 'work-by' on the old Arcadia immediately."

Then another long pause as he swept something intangible off his desk and continued.

"Perhaps a few weeks up here will do you good. Then you could join the Queen Mary."

His tired voice faded and Doug had no idea that his salary had increased by the minute. Almost stooped yet surprisingly tall the Superintendent rose from his chair wearily, grinned and placed his hand upon his new recruit's shoulder. They shook hands and Doug left, excited by the outcome, and the new adventure that lay ahead.

Attentive, Qantas Stewardess April Showers' night shift curlers now back in place was drawn back to Doug unaccountably sound asleep but snoring. Dimmed the cabin lights, relaxed his seat belt and gently covered him with up market paper thin but effective woolen blankets.

Comatose, Doug continued his remission by retreating even further back in time. Back to the day he completed his apprenticeship and left the Shipyard's womb after a row with management. Slung his hook and begun life as a Car Salesman with 'Mac's of Ambleside; mentored by his very good friend the Pie Lady, four doors up from 123. She had agreed to let him use her phone and would accept calls from prospective clients.

Part of his deal with the Pie lady was from time to time changed to suit her needs. She had something special on the side, a middle aged Butcher who exchanged favors for supplies of best top side mince. Their treasured moments timed to coincide when all her pies were sold and prioritized a lift half way to Whitehaven. It was about the time Doug had an appointment with a serious Vet class A Surgeon in Kirkby who desired a brand new car preferably black, incognito. Maybe catch up and see seldom seen Ethel Patterson who lived at Parton outside Whitehaven. Perhaps she had news from London? Maybe her scholarship had finally arrived?

Overhead black skies, omnipotent and ragged as Doug thrust Mac's 1938 Austin 16 northwards. Soon he would try to sell it for more than eighty quid, anything over eighty quid he could keep as commission. The Pie Lady all demure, powdered up; uncomfortable in impractical high heeled shoes, twisted nylon stockings. Far too much mascara around her eyes. The Duddon flecked with waves, Doug spun right for Traveler's Rest, then left at the Pub and climbed the steep winding road. Foraged through and over old somnolent former battlegrounds sparse wind-swept all buggered up Cumbrian moors, Seascale not yet in tights far below.

Once at the summit his lusty Pie Lady braced by gale force winds shimmied to the parked Singer van. Inside, the pale jubilant face of her balding lover, bespectacled, impeccably suited Flynn Errol, his louder than louder tie in disarray already savaged. Doug arranged to meet them after mad passionate love some hours later inside a popular Whitehaven Pub. Say around three, her in great form, then back to her Gumption Pie Shop, one hour before her reliable, unsuspecting William swept through their front door with flowers.

Doug's brief period of monetary success as a car salesman, had entitled him to dine out at the Lakeside Hotel and take lunch at a leisurely pace. He had really hit it off with 'Mac; always slouched inside

Michael Stockdale

his office never without an ex-RAF tie, battered air crew leather jerkin, thick heavy corduroy trousers and desert boots whenever Doug turned up. All 'Mac's family had immigrated to Canada. His large office cluttered by photographs of vintage cars and somewhere a photograph of Wing Commander 'Mac and crew posed alongside a Lancaster Bomber taken during WW2. One small family photograph showed his smiling Mam and Dad outside their Newcastle terraced house with their children and 'Mac as the eldest son in uniform.

His first opening words never changed, usually with a searching smile and some kind of reinforcement

"Do we have a sale Douglas? You must go to Church Douglas, at least once a week. You'll find more customers there than you can poke a stick at, if you do."

'Mac did not smoke or drink and rarely spoke about Madge the Nurse who had nursed him after he crash-landed somewhere in Kent. Her faded photograph kept in his shabby wallet out of sight. Madge had married another and both died hand in hand in Montgomery's desert.

Doug always nodded his head in agreement but when the old man became moribund he would relate stories about his Pie Lady's amours to generate a laugh. Or tell him a joke, or at least something humorous to lessen the morbidity which often shrouded the lonely old man. 'Mac had no family of his own and very few friends, his ex-RAF pals had either passed away or were about to. It was inevitable during their brief association that he would treat Doug as if he was his son; he after all enjoyed the lad's enthusiasm, corny jokes; admired the lad's candid outlook and was envious of his youthful optimism. 'Mac's long weather beaten face invariably showed some regret when it became time for Doug to hit the road. 'Mac was slowly dying from cancer and had not told a soul.

Doug's catch up with Ethel Patterson in Parton would prove brief. Her ambition was always to be professional singer. At first sight she had come over well with naturally black curly hair, good teeth and freckles, but saddled with thick red ankles preferred long dresses. She was an attractive short in the leg girl with an unknown figure, cadged cash for cigarettes or beer. Pleaded poverty from the first day they had met, always short of readies. Her ambition was to land a role in a West End musical, less than that did not count. There was little or no romance in their association, her heart shielded by a tough veneer. Occasional company yes but predictable; her token laugh insincere, or hollow whenever they had met or parted.

Her Dad had answered his knock and invited him in. One door closed another opened by the old man's three or four deep bronchial coughs. Ethel surrounded by stained damp falling down walls, had smiled in Doug's direction. Soprano Ethel sprawled on an old bruised settee beside her feet sheets of music, one overflowing cigarette ash tray smoldered.

"I've got it and I'm out of cigarettes. I need a beer," she screamed.

Her important letter had arrived. She had been awarded a Music scholarship after all. Her proud Dad had wheezed as if an out of tune

Michael Stockdale

accordion, worked down the Pit all his life and it more than showed. To celebrate the very same day Doug on demand went and borrowed his Grandfather's BSA motorbike, Ethel's favorite mode of transport. Once aboard she demanded a quick symbolic ride through Parton's Market. Doug unaware she had climbed up off the pillion and stood spread-eagled as if she was Jesus Christ Superstar; bold as brass cried,

"Fuck you all," two fingers of each hand extended to all startled shoppers. An incident not missed by her ashamed mother, a volunteer cleaner at Parton's church.

Drowsy eyed, Doug awoke 35,000 feet up where the air was thin outside pleased his fancy suit had withstood the test. He had slept through the casual entrance of jostling fellow passengers Qantas timed to coincide with the sounds of sticks, tap, tap, tapping accompanied by the haunting sound of didgeridoo's from the intercom. Dreamed on as primitive colors and sounds blended with the movement of other 'tribes' as they passed through his first class compartment.

He had slept for over an hour and it took him some time to adjust. Soon a relieved April Showers towered above him, contained her powerful bodily fluids, she needed a fuck, with French champagne and fussed. She did not mention the colorful language used during his disturbed sleep. His voyage back in time had raised eye brows.

Doug went and freshened up in the bathroom occupied with D'Arcy Duggan the only Australian he had befriended as a lad. The man he had tracked down on the day before he left Tarn Manor with one change of clothes, spare cash and travelers checks. To his knowledge D'Arcy lived in Brisbane and ran a small engineering consultancy. Doug had wired an open ended invitation with his flight details with a closing note,

"Maybe they could catch up!"

Some years had passed since Australians Commander James Bond Duggan and family arrived in Gumption and blended quietly into the community without a fanfare or introduction in NWEM's Editorial. Tactfully prepared the way and set up home in modest middle income Runners Park. Enrolled their children at the local Grammar School and signed up son D'Arcy for an engineering apprenticeship. The Commander's next assignment; four Mine-Sweepers commissioned by the Royal Australian Navy near to completion in the Shipyard.

Saturday night at St. Matthew's Church Hall dance, sixteen year old D'Arcy Duggan and bronzed, big breasted older sister Sheila paid one and sixpence each to gain admission and made an instant impression. Douglas V for Victor Warrington in his father's best tweed jacket took an immediate fancy to Sheila's gigantic breasts, but was pushed away by William Mussel, Grammar School's champion shot-putter. Never say die Doug was the first one in for the evening's finale, "The Yearning Saunter" used his nous and conned Sheila into a Sunday stroll down to Gumption's Abbey. One Sunday afternoon in Runner's Park, Doug washed to his waist and out to impress took 123's bull-terrier along, tough as teak Sheila bit Doug's tongue during their only kiss near the Abbey's Amphitheatre. Packed him in on their first date and blamed his dog who had savaged her coat with his muddy paws despite his protest,

Michael Stockdale

"It was nothing to do with him."

Gumption's track record in building warships in those far off days was standard fare and served as an introduction to different cultures. Venezuelan and Argentinian sailors chased and impregnated local married or single ladies. French lads were too broke to entertain or fuck anyone. English tars kept sex in-house climbed and promenaded anything accessible including the balcony on Saturday nights at Public Hall. But nobody knew what to expect when and if Duggan's Australian crew finally descended.

Time passed and at long last the commissioning of the Shipyard's Australian bound 'Wombat, Koala, Dingo and Digger,' Mine-Sweepers arrived as did hordes of rowdy Australian sailors. Duggan's crews, once ashore, were never sober. Their favorite patch was behind The Junction Pub near the Strand, not far from Doug's parent's house in Lord Street. And here they would drink like skunks. Squat, spew up and roll in vomit. Then on Saturday nights commandeer the Rink Dance floor, squat down drunk anywhere in large groups; piss and vomit in Dance Hall corners, too many, far too many to throw out for bouncer Frank to handle.

Doug had no idea what to expect in Australia. He was one of many tens of thousands of UK Radio listeners who did not know much about

"My name is Bill Kerr. I've come all the way from Australia and I've only got two minutes," recorded at noon on BBC Radio.

Tales from Planet Gumption

Folk instead took comfort and relied on feedback from popular UK performers who mocked its convict heritage, arid landscape and bronzed athletic Sheila's. 1964 was not George Orwell's world as yet. When Australian crooner Frank Ifield yodeled his way across the British Isles with unabashed good health and teeth he remembered YOU. Joined up straight away and enlisted in the Antipodes invasion. Doug had liked Frank's songs, only his Dad's dog had protested.

Tarn Manor's representative finished up his very first Scotch, discarded his perceived parochial Sydney Morning Herald and slept again cosseted by casual acquaintances. When he awoke he had company. A short well rounded affable tubby man dressed in khaki jungle fatigues and long necked rubberized boots. The man perspired freely and used a large black and white checkered handkerchief to wipe the sweat away. Blamed his phobia about flying and within minutes consumed an astonishing amount of liquor to fight it. Within just five minutes conversation, this vital short middle aged man struck Doug as being opinionated, both garrulous and volatile. Each sentence strung by together by the word "fucking" and absurd gesticulations from his exceptionally long arms, with few movements from his gleaming bald head but many from his expressive large blue eyes. He introduced himself as Dave de Mito, an American Geologist based in London's Chancery Lane who was off to assay Papua New Guinea's Ok river for gold. Laughed heartily when Doug told him his first stop would be Brisbane. Dave had been there many times and said it was a SOB one horse town. And yes, he knew of Doctor Biltong but hedged on details. This obtuse flat one liner filed and rated classified in Doug's head.

Michael Stockdale

Doug awoke several times during the flight and thought of raging twang a twang now contrite Rachel. She had contacted him and apologized for her behavior. It seemed appropriate that she should join him for lunch at Heathrow's restaurant before he left. He was astute enough to view her acumen as an asset and that he oddly enough had benefited from his perchance of social cripples; his indelible weakness. With that in mind he decided to give her one more chance to retain their friendship. Scarred for life by her ancient kettle, he decided to take her on side as his keep in touch UK Public Relation's Officer. Pound for pound, cast in steel perhaps his best decision yet.

When Doug stepped on his first piece of Australian terra firma it was in Darwin to be greeted by a blinding huge blue sky, so vast it appeared bottomless. He joined the queue outside Immigration and stood inside a natural void absorbed by an immense silence. On either side or whichever way he looked, all he could see was an empty disappearing horizon. Immigration was a simple fibro hut or shed, here he was confronted by a giant of a man in a wide high crowned broad rimmed Stetson who ticked boxes and welcomed him and others to OZ. Then another flight but this time by a much smaller and crowded domestic aircraft, far below its distorted shadow flowed seamlessly over a vast red desert land like a scrap of paper; blown by winds perhaps from south east Asia. Did they land first in Sydney or later in Brisbane, Doug had not a clue?

Somewhere along the line elusive Dave de Mito vanished. Definitely large country town Brisbane according to their pilot, it was time to test the water. The passengers disembarked slowly as if an old wine poured from a Viennese cut glass decanter. No one hurried or pushed, for many it was the end of their journey and there at the bottom of the gangway, he recognized now beefy D'Arcy Duggan. The same old D'Arcy, mouth partly open called a grin, yellow teeth, tousled hair, everything about him over relaxed and untidy mimicked crooner Frank Ifield,

"I remember youu. You old bastard! How are yah?" grabbed Doug by his shoulders, "How long is it now?"

Both were around the same age, D'Arcy tanned and sported a pot-belly. To him Doug looked whiter than white, same old mop but shorn down to his scalp, his body surprisingly firm and hard. Doug smiled broadly but his eyes suggested he was somewhere else. Too many distractions the intangible weight of responsibility had left their mark.

"Hello sailor," it was Qantas's Eiffel Tower, Flight Attendant April Showers light and cheerful dressed to the nines and looked magnificent.

"What?" Doug spun around gasped, "Hey, What's happening?" Genuinely, pleased.

"Bugger off!" piped D'Arcy's mother, an elegant tiny wizened creature decked out in paisley blue with small dog restrained by one gloved hand.

April glowered ignored the old cow, retained her decorum and slipped her card to Doug.

Michael Stockdale

"I'm camped out for a week at the Bellevue. Maybe we can do Brisbane?" Doug puzzled by D'Arcy's mother's caustic retort agreed.

"Good idea. Why not? I'll give you a bell," and watched her stomp away.

Doug had not seen Pearl since in her house at Runner's Park. She had aged considerably and smelt of booze when she kissed him. Two short muscled men in rabbit skin hats then came out of nowhere and said "Good day mate." Introduced as D'Arcy's two older brothers Doug had never met. Both tensed their biceps like body builder comedian Milano.

It was extremely hot and humid. Australia's southern hemisphere sun attacked Doug's northern lights and fried his neck with gusto. Take a memo; he would have to buy a hat. "Doug should drive," squeaked demanding tremulous Pearl as if he knew the way. Her grey scrupulously clean etched Holden car two tone automatic passive to one side, no obvious architectural statements outside his window, it seemed a barren place. Doug would not recall who drove the car, or much about the vista except it appeared much the same on route. Wooden houses with verandas painted all the same. D'Arcy's house in Crumpet Road was a large rambling timber relic hoisted skywards, seated; anchored to crude black stumps. Several empty carports at the rear. One space occupied by an old green Dodge truck; loaded up with junk appeared neglected belonged to D'Arcy's Grandfather an unwashed reminder of his ardent past.

Pearl showed him through to her bedroom. Old fashioned veneered timber wardrobes lined one wall. On top, a variety of old and new suitcases and suspended from the ceiling an oscillating fan which wafted round and round, kindly offered it as his bedroom for the night. Doug tested Pearl's toilet inside her plastic sheeted bathroom, its toilet pedestal remarkably close to a short rectangular bathtub, shaded by a thin see through floral plastic curtain. The bath doubled as a shower and was very small. The rest of the house chopped up into three or four small one or two roomed flats. Outside and again at the rear, Pearl's remarkably ancient tenants in their pajamas or nighties watered small plots of garden oblivious of everyone. The direct opposite to the world he had left. Another planet and another era, Doug hit the hay jet lagged and out of it.

Dawn and piercing sun arrived very early in the morning, outside an awful racket. Doug wide awake waded through Pearl's museum of discarded family items. The corridor outside jammed with more mounds of furniture even an old iron single bed. He squeezed past to the open front door to source the racket and was met by the sight of a wall of traffic in Crumpet Road. Stalled or hampered by large partially open antiquated and colorful noisy electric trams. These mechanized monoliths trundled past Pearl's front door day and night, three times as noisy as the Council buses that stopped outside 123.

Pearl's bed was huge. He had slept well, except when disturbed by someone who crawled in and snuggled up. At first he thought he was dreaming or perhaps it was one of six Pearl's cats, surely not the feeble frame of Pearl? My God, the old bag had wrapped her legs around his body. He delicately detached, grabbed a pillow and blanket and took up residence on the floor. Bitten by mosquitos who buzzed around his head, these local lads along with Pearl had interrupted his night's sleep. Doug failed miserably to either maim or kill the enemy, leapt silently around the bedroom not quite naked. It was a futile exercise but alerted Pearl who produced a coil of compacted highly scientific cow shit. Lit one single match and produced a toxic stink tantamount to war and left him to it.

Two days in and Doug was still recovering from his long flight when in walked Wally, D'Arcy's short fat bluff eldest brother said "Good day." Then joined them all for breakfast and invited Doug along to meet the Manager of his Bank of NSW. Why? Doug did not know. His Australian Bank was ANZ but he allowed himself to be introduced to Foreman material, hair parted in the middle, greased with exotic discounted alligator hair lotion shifty Gus the Bank Manager. Sneered, not impressed.

"How much would you like to deposit Mr. Warrington?"

"Nothing, thank you very much," said Doug.

Wally grimaced: Disgusted, made a mental note; perspired. Short of a quid and in need of a dollar, told Pearl he was going to sell their old Dodge truck. But Pearl would have none of it and told him it was not for sale.

Then when Doug felt chipper, his jetlag gone he went walkabout. Found his legs and braved the heat. Climbed aboard a City bound Tram to explore Brisbane. Unable to cope with the Tram's unpredictable movements, collided with a wayward canvas curtain. Landed softly, cushioned by two pairs of meaty female thighs seated opposite. Misinterpreted as outright lust, by an elderly female passenger dressed for bowling; raged with her parasol screamed

"Pull *your bloody* horns yah dirty minded bastard."

Rang the bell and alighted still agitated at Blue Hills.

All roads led to Rome, minutes later the driver yelled, "Next stop Town Hall." Outside the window the facsimile of Gumption's except that it came with mounted towering Imperial statues, out of place African Lions and to Doug's knowledge the luxury of a full-time Mayor. A very long way from Gumption's part-time equivalent, white haired still nimble Union man Alfred the Gun-Shop Welder.

Directly opposite sat City Square and across the road his next abode, Lennon's Hotel. Lathered in sweat he wandered in, nearly swooned from its air-conditioned icy blast and confirmed his booking.

"Would Mr. Warrington care to view his Penthouse?"

"No thanks, I'm sure it will do me fine."

Sensitive to Pearl and D'Arcy's generous hospitality Doug had already considered remaining at Crumpet Road. But then who else would or could cope with dog shit on the carpet, mosquitos, noise from feral trams and lack of air conditioning? Sentiment aside he was in Australia on business. The decision made. That was that.

He then spent a while, as was his policy and communicated with strangers. Escaped the heat inside air-conditioned shops and chewed the fat with almost anyone. In particular, with shaved head salesman Harold inside an Edward Street Camera Shop. Lead singer in a band more inclined to talk about his next gig rather than attempt to sell another camera.

Not so the sharp as a tack car salesman in Seeger's Queen Street used car-yard when Doug strolled in and admired a modified pristine FJ Holden up for sale. Sized him up straight away, watched as Doug slid his hand along the vehicle's crimped roof gutter. Grabbed his elbow was emphatic

"Nope mate, that vehicle was never rolled."

"Bullshit, Sunshine," laughed Doug half-heartedly and walked away.

The decision made Doug returned to Crumpet Road. Packed his bags, prepared his gifts. It was time to leave and do the business. Demonstrated his appreciation to randy Pearl with orchids and hand wrapped large box of Swiss chocolates. D'Arcy eagerly accepted the bottle of Scotch but was reluctant to accept that Doug was not a migrant. In Brisbane on business only and would be around for at least two weeks. And yes, Doug would like to see his office as soon as possible.

Happy days, Lennon's receptionist reminded Doug of Agnes, pert and clear minded. Her fancy name was Augustine, bored as hell with Brisbane. Fluttered eyelashes, patted an imaginary bun rattled Doug. Dear Agnes did much the same. Outside the precinct Fig Trees shaded most roads into town. Most commandeered by large unwieldy Holden's or V8 Ford motor cars. Bustled across Brisbane's River, via old steel Made in Scotland fabricated bridges. For some strange reason Doug sensed the river as threatening. Its width was vast. Its appearance disguised as taciturn. Colored brown, all powerful, yet to him beneath its surface it seemed ill at ease.

His first appointment was with Lode contact Dr. Biltong in his suite of rooms in Eagle Street's only high rise office building. The 'Doctor' was not a Doctor professionally, but liked the title, wore his Homburg hat in doors and smoked a large cigar. Spoke in broken English sounded more like a Yank, but dressed in muted colors; khaki lightweight trousers, matching Safari lightweight jacket, plain shirt no tie and invested in elastic sided squatter boots. Biltong stood in an empty Reception when Doug arrived and introduced himself.

"How do my name in Doug Warrington. I believe you're expecting me?"

"Ah, yes!" Biltong grunted, avoided Doug's eyes and waved his cigar. Was not impressed, sniffed.

"Do yah mind? No? Well, I've heard a lot about you. I've not seen hide or hair of Lode for years." Spat on the floor continued.

Michael Stockdale

"Do you prefer to be called Mr. Warrington or Douglas?"

Sneezed out aloud and rummaged through his pockets. His eyes watered.

"Bastard Hay Fever, somewhere I have my medication. Pardon me."

Sprinkled out a small portion of white powder from a narrow plastic cylinder onto a sheet of A4 paper and plied it to his nose. Inhaled, gnashed his teeth

"Wow, now where was I? Ever been to Poland? I hate fucking Brisbane, Newcastle and Rome." Exhaled deeply, "That's very good shit. Forgive me I have a client and others waiting. Read the Courier Mail and make yourself comfortable."

Biltong's consulting engineering practice had won a contract on the construction of an oil refinery down at Lytton, an outer suburb of Brisbane. The Doctor was supposed to be Lode's ears and eyes primarily in Brisbane, but struck Doug as an atypical businessman and 'in your face' dope head. Not too subtle with it either because of what had to be a contrived 'meeting.' Doug, a total stranger witnessed through an open door as he waited in Reception. For one thing the office space was huge but lacked the usual furniture, except for one long naked table and several occupied chairs outside his office. The Doc' kept Doug waiting for what he interpreted as a calculated twenty minutes as the group of men sat around and openly discussed their next project.

From what Doug discerned it was a discussion which centered on the

Tales from Planet Gumption

flotation of a new company to promote the leaching of gold from tailings of a disused Gympie Gold Mine. Their conversation entirely based on high density lucrative samples provided by Biltong. One of the men, bearded with a thin falsetto voice represented an assumed well-respected mining finance authority Logan PLC affiliated with national publication Mining Mint Options. Shares would start at $2.00 each. The pantomime lasted about fifteen minutes and no one questioned Doug about his presence. In fact and to the contrary, when they had completed their business they came over and cordially introduced themselves. Then as if on cue The Doctor materialized from his office and waved Doug in with apologies for the delay. Behind his large desk was a magnified map of Queensland dotted by tiny plastic flags. On an adjacent wall a simple blackboard covered with small sketches and mathematical formulae. From Doug's perspective he had no idea how much Lode had invested in Biltong's resources but from what he had just witnessed, intuitively it came over as a proposition that relied on greed.

In parting Biltong said Doug could call in anytime at his Lytton Refinery Site and would keep him posted on his latest project. That night Doug dined with Qantas Flight Attendant April Showers at the Belleview's OK Corral Restaurant. Sid Monty, the English singer performed and crooned as they ate. Later, they slipped upstairs to April's room for privacy. Unknown to Doug and within minutes, April slyly drugged his coffee. When he awoke, his head throbbed as if a hangover, his body bruised and battered her on top out of her brain totally knackered. Doug slid from under her voluptuous torso, breathed a long sigh of relief, showered for nigh on twenty minutes. Crept out of Room 362 left the 'Do not disturb,' sign outside her door with fifty dollars attached.

Isolated from the main stream he was learning fast. Three drug issues in a row were grim statistics to the man who worked off the odds. Biltong treated Cocaine like confectionary. Prescription drugs Pearl appeared similarly inclined and as for April God only knows? So the odds were that drugs were rife in OZ. As for Gumption, as usual he had no idea. Now ravenous he returned to Lennon's Hotel and ordered full English breakfast and ate in his room. Read up on the Stock Market and Sydney job vacancies in the latest Australian edition of the Sydney Morning Herald newspaper and ringed in those of interest. From what he had heard Sydney was a thriving metropolis and the place to visit when in Australia. Meanwhile he tried on his new, made in Italy lightweight suit, one pair of recommended elastic sided R T Simpson's handmade boots purchased at Wells, ten minutes away. Outside his building, the temperature was 36 degrees Celsius and soaring.

Today was marked down for a visit to D'Arcy's Valley consultancy. Located in the middle of Brisbane's China Town, a neglected, rundown part of the City well-known for its Chinese restaurants and underworld characters it attracted. His office was on the second floor of a three story plain brick building accessed by interior stairs. At first sight it was the closest thing to Gumption Island's tenement blocks, differentiated by a myriad of rusted air-conditioners attached to its outside walls, locked faceless windows shaded by limp or broken blinds.

The cardboard sheet stuck to D'Arcy's entrance was brief in content.

Tales from Planet Gumption

'This office will be closed on Thursdays and Fridays. Personal interviews will be conducted only on Mondays. Please leave your details with reception. D'Arcy Recruitment regrets this inconvenience.'

Doug tapped on the door's frosted glass window and entered. D'Arcy stood to the rear deep in thought reading a file. His hair now slicked back, no longer smoked instead chewed on an unlit cigarette.

"Hey-up old son," said Doug, "What's the latest?"

"Good to see yah mate," D'Arcy howled.

Doug closed the door and came straight to the point.

"I thought you ran an engineering consultancy and not a recruitment agency?"

D'Arcy frowned half muttered more to himself than his audience.

"Times change fast around here sport and an ear to the ground keeps me posted. I'll explain everything over lunch."

Close on noon. The arterial road outside D'Arcy's office was thick with bumper to bumper car and truck traffic, narrow pavements crowded with mainly Asian faces. Instead of oxygen, heavy diesel combined with petrol fumes and spiced aromas from small takeaways. Suddenly D'Arcy without any explanation grabbed Doug and shoved him into an empty shop doorway. The sudden crack of a loud explosion, D'Arcy's building engulfed in flames. Thick black plumes of acrid smoke filtered slowly over Fortitude Valley's Asian community. Created panic drowned by sirens from several fire engines.

"Hey-up," cried Doug, "That was your office."

D'Arcy did not answer.

"What the fuck is going on?" hissed Doug.

D'Arcy ignored. Pushed ahead against the crowd of onlookers and once out of view, hailed a taxi and told the driver to take them to the Crook Hotel. Then, guided his guest to an open courtyard cluttered with plastic tables and chairs, smiled sheepishly called out to Priscilla the Pub's one of several transsexual barmaids.

"Two pots of Tooth's luv, two medium rare T-bones with sides. I hope yah like your steak medium rare old friend. Get this beer down yah, there's money to be made in the recruitment business, welcome to the world of bloody Biltong."

It was in the Crook Hotel's courtyard that D'Arcy confided about his latest venture and placed an odd looking scrap of paper on the Pub's glassed-top table.

"Found this little beauty under my door this morning," and pushed it towards Doug. It read, 'Vacate your office by midday.'

Tales from Planet Gumption

"Christ Almighty, a message in a bottle. Did you inform the police?" gasped Doug and nodded to D'Arcy.

"Yep," they weren't interested. Our building's empty. I took all my gear out yesterday just in case."

D'Arcy claimed his main competitor was Biltong Hire another sideline involved with Government contracts to reduce State overheads. Doug groaned inwardly now prepared for almost anything. So what was Biltong's game? From Doug's experience in Real Estate he was more likely to believe that inner City property was extremely valuable. And from what he had seen in Brisbane's Fortitude Valley it was up for grabs for anyone. Biltong's tentacles seemed everywhere; staff recruitment, real estate and mining. Particularly, phony floats of disused gold or silver mines, where the underlying concept appeared tempting and undeniably feasible.

Next day an article appeared in Brisbane's Courier Mail which referred to a gas leak as the culprit to the Valley explosion. The damage to the building described as a minor weakening of its foundations and was not as substantial as first thought. Mr. K. Kong a prominent Singapore investor in the area had in past months submitted a proposal to build a luxury block of residential flats on the site. Council advised that his proposal was accepted prior to the explosion. Doug did not need the brain of brain surgeon to dot the eyes or cross his tees. Theoretically at least, D'Arcy's Recruitment Agency appeared to have merit. Doug decided to rent an Avid car with the intention to check out Miserable Deposits on Queensland's Gold Coast. Called Dick Barton-Special

Projects to tell him he had landed and was on his way.

Brisbane's city boundaries seemed huge and bore no comparison to Gumptions. The Gold Coast road from Brisbane turned out to be poorly maintained and badly cambered with rough edges. It knocked the shit out of his Holden car's suspension and he soon found out his vehicle was not safe to drive over sixty miles an hour. Bumped and jogged almost to death he stopped outside a roadside shed, overhead the sign read Percy's Famous Pies. Once inside, another sign read 'Only customers can use the toilet.' Percy the Pie man was not difficult to miss, blocked the doorway with his belly; another import but from Preston, married to Kylie who manned the chip pan born in Keswick. As soon as Percy opened his mouth it was as if he had never left England.

"Now then Sunshine," he boomed, "Anyone who's been to Preston and stood on Preston's Railway Station would agree that the only sign visible from the platform was that of my Dad's pie shop."

"Dead on," agreed Doug, "Any mushy pea's old son?"

"Is the Pope a Catholic?"

"Aye, well he was when I last saw him."

Doug's pie and chips tasted dreadful, he doused down with Coke then asked if he could use Percy's toilet.

"Take this key attached to this mallet," said the whale. "You'll find it round the back and go easy on the paper."

"How much do I owe you?" Doug enquired.

Exasperated truly uncomfortable, when he returned; forced to hold on because Percy's toilet had no door.

"In old currency, seven and six, but five bob to you."

"Take this 'pound' towards that monument out the back and we'll call it quits."

Doug blustered, stamped out thoroughly desperate, placed his memento, the Pie man's mallet and key on the passenger seat.

Half an hour later he parked outside Southport's RSL, pushed aside two elderly arguing drinkers, crowned the RSL's pristine toilet and left the mallet and key with lost and found at reception. Percy's Famous Pies and phone number emblazoned on the mallet's handle.

Doug's open appointment was with Dick Barton, Special Projects, officially the Design Office Manager at Miserable Deposits. The company was one of a small group of sand-mining operators in Queensland. Its office and workshop located on an industrial estate not far from Southport. At first sight the entrance to Miserable Deposit's low set office building was neat and tidy, fronted by a spacious covered parking area and driveway. Externally it featured large panoramic tinted windows which overlooked what appeared to be artificial textured lawns.

Michael Stockdale

Reception was immediately inside and to the left. Doug entered and reported to the middle aged woman breast feeding a baby, hands covered with copper rings seated behind the counter. She was brisk and made an internal call then asked him to take a seat whispered confidentially

"Mr. Barton is in conference but would be available in ten minutes."

Doug sat down and took in the overly silent air conditioned surroundings. The building's interior strictly conservative and somber, deafened by dark brown laminated wooden panels. Reminiscent of St. Egbert's Church devoid of parishioners. Ten minutes passed, half an hour and Doug asleep jolted into gear by a strident, enthusiastic voice.

"Good day, good day Douglas isn't it? Sorry to keep you waiting. Has anyone offered tea or coffee? No, well we'll soon fix that."

Doug grasped the thin man's proffered sun spotted hand, and felt another land on his shoulder.

"I'm Dick Barton Special Projects come on down to my office."

Doug followed the agile sprinter at galloping pace, past and through glass cubicles then into a large room full of drawing boards and bobbing heads. The sprinter waved his arms, issued instructions on the hop and finally guided him through into his office.

"Take a chair while I fix up my desk."

Tales from Planet Gumption

Grasped a large open family sized Holy Bible, bookmarked his place and placed it on top of a nearby bookcase then rattled off numerous questions.

"We have tea or coffee, with or without sugar. We've got the lot, biscuits, chocolate or whole-meal? Hang-on, what about a nice vanilla slice? They're fresh in today."

Then out of the blue an abrupt irate tall bald headed man inside a white tee-shirt emblazoned with 'Peace.' Baggy khaki shorts, large opened toed rope sandals groveled at Barton's door, slid into Dick's tiny space grated.

"My apologies mate, can I have my Bible back?"

"No problems," said Dick and heaved the massive tome towards his visitor.

"Read Revelations, I've already bookmarked it and bugger off," turned to Doug with a quizzical eye, "So when can you start?"

"Sorry?" bleated Doug and caught the strong whiff of marijuana in from the corridor.

Now dumbfounded he weighed up the possibilities that Dick Barton Special Projects was crackers surrounded by chaos and on Pot.

Michael Stockdale

"That idiot bloke was our consulting engineer. That man spent six weeks valuable time on Cape Snapper's expansion and we are no bloody closer to completion since when he started. Anyhow I've just fired him. What say lunch?"

Lode's introductory letter to Miserable Deposits had included a brief summary of Doug's background and his itinerary. Barton had underlined that Lode intended to expand its overseas operations and may utilize some of MD's patented equipment. In addition Lode wrote 'it would be appreciated if their representative had access to their operations.' Doug had not forgotten this added clause and agreed to a guided tour after lunch.

Barton drove a bright red Alfa Romeo green clover sticker. Its rear seat filled with assorted golf clubs. A smiling plastic Buddha swung from the rear view mirror in time with a nodding toy koala that lay against the car's rear window. Suddenly a bearded man weighed down by a large wooden cross across his back blocked their way.

"Hey Jesus, you're leaving early then?" cried Dick from his open window. "What's the route, same as usual?"

"Yep," replied the bearded man, "Down through Surfers Paradise to Miami and then back again. Praise the Lord."

Doug shook his head from side to side. The wheel attached to the base of the wooden cross had just fallen off.

Tales from Planet Gumption

"You'll get used to our religious endeavors Douglas," yodeled Barton, "The bloke who designed our separation plant is Jesus's Dad."

Doug picked at his T-bone steak as Dick Barton enthused about the business opportunities in Queensland. It was during lunch when Doug made a serious management decision and nipped out to send a wire to Lode.

'Update: Miserable Deposits contacted. The 'Doc is into disused gold and silver mines. Best Regards, DVW'

When they returned Doug was introduced to Luke Warm the Drawing Office supervisor and Dick left them to it. Luke's office was full of posters that advertised alternative life-styles in a place called Watson Creek. An incredibly thin young/old man with long lank blond streaked with grey uncombed hair to his shoulders he fingered as he spoke. Said little, smiled too much, was laid back and bearded, dressed in faded denim. His office stank of weed, his breath of high octane petrol. But appearances proved to be deceptive. Luke turned out to be esthetically, almost over genial but was an obvious authority on sand mining. Doug graciously declined home-made cigarettes, requested and was given copies of MD typical sand mining arrangements to take and study for easy reference.

Doug hung around until 'morning tea.' Then together they wandered off and joined the other draftsmen outside Main Office. Here, Luke introduced him to fellow travelers in the trade. Most were 'Ten pound migrants' from the British Isles, one from Manchester and all were under contract to MD. The main topic of conversation dwelled on 'piles' or remedies to stop bleeding. Religion too had its place, Luke the ardent non-believer, curried favors from those who prayed and on the side sold Amway products which specialized on weight reduction. Luke's missus fifteen stone and climbing.

Dazed by weed and repetitive chat Doug retreated back and popped into Dick's hale fellow well met Office. Dick surprised and confused to hear he was leaving.

"Going? I thought you were here for a while to help us out."

"Hang on," laughed Doug, "I'll be back but not on a drawing board. You misunderstood Lode's memo. I came here to look around and touch base."

"Well, there go," Dick grinned and stretched out a hand, "I haven't a clue what's going on. So we'll see you when we see you?"

"Correct, we'll be in touch. I'm off back to Brisbane and I'll give you a bell when next in town. Thanks a lot for your co-operation it was appreciated."

Doug climbed into his Avid rented car sat and pondered on what he had seen, sedated by weed and religion and a very long way from the green fields of England. D'Arcy's great adventure brimmed with fire and smoke, the elusive 'Doc who ferreted with gold and silver tailings. Raped by an elderly Qantas Amazon! Doug had plenty to think about on his return journey to Brisbane. Next stop Lennon's reception and most definitely not Preston Percy's Famous Pies. Then changed his mind, popped in and confronted Percy,

"One question, why the mallet attached to your toilet key, when it hasn't got a bloody door?"

"To kill the cockroaches Sunshine and I'm one mallet down."

For one second, Doug believed him.

On his way back Doug decided to check out 'Doc's hideaway in Lytton. His Avid car came with a map of Brisbane and outlying areas. Lytton was located near Fisherman's Island and the surrounding countryside appeared relatively flat and uninteresting or forgotten. Unable to see any substantial buildings either side en route to the site he remained on Lytton Road until he saw the sign "Civil & Petroleum Projects" parked beside an old household bath with one tap next to a fence and primitive gateway. In the distance one small prefabricated tin shed.

Doug drove gingerly across the paddock and parked the Holden beside the shed. In almost every direction stretched acres and acres of unoccupied land. The door was ajar and he was met a wave of intense heat generated from its unlined shell. Inside, the space was sparsely furnished with two desks, one phone, and two bulky loose packages of engineering drawings. No bloody electricity connected and no chairs to sit on. So this was the 'Doc's big site operation? It was puzzling and contrary to the information Doug had received. The sudden hard knock from the fat diesel engine of an oncoming truck as it eased up outside next to the shed. A loud raucous laugh, he had a visitor and stepped out of the oven.

"What the fuck is *your* problem?"

The rasping question came from a middle aged man who wore a Stetson and chewed on an unlit cigar as he struggled with a small portable refrigerator.

"Sorry? Doug said testily, "The 'Doc said I was expected. I know who I am, but who the fuck are you?"

"Me? I'm the fucking Project Manager on this site buddy. And I don't take shit from anyone so wing it or lend a hand with the refrigerator on the truck."

"OK, let's do it," said Doug, "But less of the bull-shit," caught one end of the refrigerator and eased it through the door. "Where do you want it?

"Next to the power point on that wall," waved a thumb muttered, "Now beat it." Perplexed, Doug did not move.

"My name's Al, *go now* you've just been fired."

The Yank or Canadian grinned, threw the cigar stub away and pulled a fresh cigar from his shirt pocket lit it, inhaled and blew smoke into Doug's face grimaced added.

"On *your* way sonny boy, like I said, whoever you are you've just been fired."

Meanwhile, the sounds of other trucks and more voices outside, most appeared to be American. Buckled belts, cowboy boots access to American Express but no Stetsons; six men entered as Doug slipped Al his business card. Inside the air soon thick with laughter and cigar smoke, followed by an intense argument about their outstanding wages where "Fuck you too," was prominent.

Then another voice, but more strident and definitely Australian hurled abuse outside and demanded to speak with the Project Manager. Al stiffened and angrily stepped out of his office to meet someone he did not know and had never met. The Managing Director of Avid stood against his chauffeur driven Caprice and to his rear his team of drivers waited inside an Answer Airways Courtesy Bus. The man from Avid was blunt.

"Your Company owes my Company a mint. I told your Managing Director Biltong an hour ago I intend to repossess all his site vehicles as of today. That means now, except for that Holden, do you wanker's understand me loud and clear?"

Doug had heard enough, sidled out and away back to the Holden. The silence from inside the shed was deafening as outside Avid issued brisk directives to his drivers. Soon nine vehicles in convoy slowly moved out of the field and followed Doug's route back to Brisbane. The car hire company's CEO's parting shot.

"Call a fucking taxi."

When Doug arrived at Lennon's Reception, the news from Lode was. 'Forget about sand mining and think about coal.' The Doc's wire arrived on the same day, 'Biltong's meeting with backers to float a Company to leach old tailings from disused Silver and Goldmines approved.'

"Big Deal," called Doug out aloud.

Disconcerted and bushed from ongoing drama, he slumped on his bed. He needed someone to talk to, when the bedside phone rang, it was sultry Rachel a million miles away.

"Hello Australia, something has popped out under the radar which may be useful to know. The British Government plans to eventually close down all or most UK coal mines."

"Oh, c'mon petal, they've gone and cancelled the bloody sand-mining project and I've only been here just over a week. I might as well give the whole damn show away."

"Wait a minute dear," she cooed. "There's more. Certain influential American interests should they get into power, and the likelihood is that they will, intend to invest heavily in China and obtain possibly lots of easily mined e.g. cheap coal from elsewhere. Think Australia. How do I know this? Daddy is a member of an exclusive City Club, and thought you should know about it."

Wearied with the chat and turn of events Doug responded gallantly.

"Tell your Dad it was appreciated and I'll think about it. I'm off to bed, phone again tomorrow pet about the same time. Sweet dreams," and hung up.

Now off the bed Doug stretched out on a divan and pondered over Keno Hill's sprawling Death Valley and it's literally tons of untouched tailings. To him it was worth a punt. He wired Lode's Head Office direct to his de facto father in law with a request. Included was a brief explanatory note on leaching and asked him to check out the owners if any, on the land and/or lease in Death Valley.

Twenty four hours later Maurice Lode leapt with joy when he captured the rights to leach Keno Hills Death Valley tailings for only a few dollars with the consummate blessings from the newly formed Yukon Government's environmental body. The value of Gumption's Barclay's Bank account in the name of Douglas V for Victor Warrington without him knowing tripled. Doug's personal file under lock and key in Maurice Lode's desk had him listed as Lode's Business Development Executive and CEO of a stalled, but optimistic well-funded sand-mining Company.

It was during breakfast three days later Doug received another but peculiar wire to call Lode Geology direct to obtain confidential detailed co-ordinates of land near two small Queensland towns named Gladstone and Moura. Two towns he would be expected to visit and assess. It also recommended he should adopt a low profile e.g. not too bright tourist etc. D'Arcy Duggan came to mind. Doug slotted him well inside that division. Anyhow Doug knew D'Arcy would be good company in any situation and knew the lay of the land.

The Drum was only dickheads drove out west in a two bob car. D'Arcy knew the territory, Doug had no idea. He agreed that D'Arcy would choose the vehicle. Not quite a Camel it came equipped with an air cooled engine, portable two gas burner stove. Table/beds, one ten gallon water tank, canvas annex, full-length roof rack with ladder. Spare batteries, independent lighting and rechargeable sockets. Curtained windows to keep the sun out, an insulated roof. It was practical but as slow as buggery.

Elated to be out of Fortitude Valley, a reformed Duggan took the second-hand VW Kombi wheel and skidded round the back of his Crumpet Road house, no need for garden gnomes, left the same old battlers as they fiddled in the garden. Drugged up in prescription mode Pearl baked a piece of topside beef, stuffed with herbs, the specialty of the house. Their host smoked 200 cigarettes, polished off one bottle of Scotch and one bottle of Sherry each week, read countless romantic paperbacks and tatted. Her tiny dog never ever house trained, still shit on the floor. All or most of it absorbed by Pearl's wall to wall in threads, multi-colored carpet. They said their cheerios and headed north.

Tales from Planet Gumption

The Pacific Highway was a national highway misnomer, full of potholes and at times extremely dangerous. Littered, by small bush towns with mandatory police station, courthouse, three Pubs, bowling-green, Masons Hall and badly attended one teacher State Schools. Bundled worker's timber cottages some unpainted or painted Queensland Railway's green with well-maintained precious lawns. Figments of the past which on another day would or could be seen as original treasures; exuded charm built in the traditional fashion; rough in texture or damned exceptional ideally with verandas. Small towns featured lonely parks but as necessities, void of people, but rarely short of toilet paper in their dry disinfected toilets. All or most had wide tree lined streets with the minimum of street lighting. Many were one street in and one street out ghost towns, one petrol bowser and takeaways.

The road to Gladstone seemed a lonely road with little traffic, haunting as dusk fell and eerie in the black of night. The utility truck that followed them mile after mile raised D'Arcy's suspicions and he urged the Kombi forward, flashed his lights with the hope it would pass. It declined and remained to their rear then moved out and then accelerated to overtake as the bullet penetrated the VW's rear window and lodged inside the dashboard. Out of character Doug moved like greased lightning and jerked the steering wheel through D'Arcy's hands. Aimed and rammed the VW's Bull-bar at the speeding utility's tailgate. Out of control the utility skidded bodily sideways and left the road. Bounced and rolled down a steep embankment then exploded within seconds. Doug stopped the VW, grabbed a torch and edged down the slope. Some distance away from the smoldering wreckage he located two blackened lifeless bodies. But noticed one door of the truck had separated and recognized the untarnished logo on its panel. It was identical to the one he had seen on Biltong's Lytton Site hut rolled his eyes murmured, "Holy shit," wended back to the stationary VW. D'Arcy, badly shaken pursed his lips responded.

"Jesus Christ. That was close. That was very fucking close. You'd better drive. I nearly shit myself when I heard that bang and heard that bullet."

Doug was thinking hard, took the wheel and kept it simple.

"We'll report this to the Gladstone Police as soon as we arrive."

At the same time, retrieved the bullet from the dashboard without any comment and did not mention the utility's logo; the less D'Arcy knew the better.

Onward to Gladstone, first stop its Police Station to report an accident. Constable Trumpet was fat and ugly. He took his time with the pencil but was obliging and thanked them kindly. He recommended the Rocky Mount Motel in town as the best motel for miles. They booked in and Doug estimated their stay would be for at least two days. The heat in Gladstone was horrific. The VW had no air-conditioning. Twenty minutes exposed to the sun nearly sent Doug blind eyed. At times he was convinced his brains had been fried to a crisp. Unlike D'Arcy who romped around like a schoolboy. Reminisced about his early days as the Gladstone's greatest lover, yet in the past and although his birthplace, he never seemed to miss it. The Rocky Mount Motel also doubled as a pub,

Tales from Planet Gumption

Gladstone had more Pubs than supermarkets.

Inside any Gladstone Pub the odds were D'Arcy would meet a friend or relative he had not seen for years. For a second incognito Doug thought perhaps D'Arcy had too many friends and relatives in Queensland. On the back seat of the Kombi lay a Surveyor's Dumpy purchased at Brisbane's Army and Navy Stores he would use to conduct an approximate survey of the area known as Barney Point nominated by Lode as best he could.

Next day they drove down to Barney Point and apart from the oppressive heat both were impressed by Gladstone's magnificent natural harbor. Visually the area of land Doug would try to survey appeared to house old holiday shacks and swimmers. Some in groups fished from a sandy beach while others swam or fished from small tin boats. It appeared to be very close to Gladstone's small business center. It occurred to Doug the land would be suitable for the storage of almost anything and knowing Lode perhaps some kind of terminal in the future. There was talk in town of a new power station and maybe new Smelter. He assumed all new construction came under the jurisdiction of Queensland State Government and Gladstone's City Council.

They roughly identified the land mass Lode had requested. But the idea behind Lode's directive seemed distinctly weird. More like a junket. Thousands of miles to do something basic did not make sense. He took one last long look at postcard picturesque Gladstone Harbor. He had seen enough and based on well-founded rumors soon scuttled their Moura visit. Changed tack and instead drove and located the town's Public

Michael Stockdale

Library. Read back-copies of the local newspaper and came across inside the Library's reference section some old Australian Geology magazines. Some of which dated back as far as 1936. It was a fool's errand. Coal deposits were identified long ago in detail. So why all the intrigue and mystery exhibited by Lode? Gossip in the local high street Pub salvaged by D'Arcy spoke of interested Brisbane based contractors. Panned as local punters up and pottering around Moura and smelled of mining. Doug made enquiries at Gladstone's City Council office who admitted there was a possibility of the construction of a proposed rail link between Moura and Barney Point, information which was readily available and common knowledge. However, some concerns had been expressed by locals against a proposed coal stockpile at Barney Point a popular beauty spot and so close to town. An area owned by a local man said to be a Gladstone chemist.

The more Doug delved the longer they stayed at the Rocky Mount Motel. Moura and Queensland's entire Bowen Basin was known untapped coal territory. It was time for lunch and they ate Chinese in town and bumped into Policeman Trumpet.

"Good day mates. That truck was stolen from an Avid car outlet by two escapees from a Brisbane watch-house. Well, there yah go, how long do yah intend to stay in Gladstone?"

D'Arcy flinched. Doug was nonplussed.

"My wife is English born and bred in a place called Coniston in the Lakes District if yah know it and I was thinking well."

Tales from Planet Gumption

Here Trumpet leaned across the table and pointed at Doug,

"Your accent is a bit like hers. We met and married last year and she's terribly homesick."

"What's her name?" asked Doug with sudden interest.

"Penelope, her mother ran the boarding house near the bridge,"

Trumpet wryly replied embarrassed by his frank admission.

'Glassy eyed Penny?' Thought Doug but dare not say it. The Policeman's eyes went watery.

"Hey. Why not dinner at our place? Yah know where I hang out and let me know see-yah."

Once Trumpet had left his chair and disappeared out of sight, Doug leaned closer to D'Arcy and modified plans.

"I reckon I'll sling my hook and head off back to Brisbane. Maybe catch a plane out of Gladstone today. You can stay here if you want. Catch up with your relatives and flog that Kombi ASAP or keep it. I'll square up the Motel and here's a few quid to cover expenses."

D'Arcy flicked through the proffered currency like a Bookie's runner, smiled and nodded his head eagerly. Doug's chair scraped against the tiled floor as he rose to his feet, and he grinned at D'Arcy's dog-like expression. Patted him on the head and laughed at his own joke.

"Maybe we'll catch up in Brisbane?"

"Too right," said D'Arcy and tapped Doug on the shoulder.

"We'll see yah in Brisbane then?"

When Doug arrived at Lennon's Hotel it was dusk. He collected but ignored the small pile of telegrams and instead soaked inside a hot tub. Then dried off and looked out over City Hall, its illuminated clock, statues, square and very little activity. Ate dinner in his suite and wondered what the hell was going on out there where nothing moved after eight at night. Before he went to sleep he read the latest editions of the Courier Mail and the industry magazine Mining Mint Options. The latter featured an article about the recent float of a new Mining Company Leach Holdings in association with Logan PLC. It included a touched-up photograph of one of the men he had met in Biltong's Eagle Street office. Logan's market analyst, prim and bearded who in very small print; described the asset as an investment with a strong and healthy future. The acting broker for all enquires was the reputable Willy Bowery-Boyes based in Queen Street, Brisbane.

Before Doug hit the hay he compiled a brief list of business opportunities and summarized it simply:

'Coal mining projects in central Queensland and rolling stock expansion from Gladstone to Moura is feasible and a distinct possibility, as is the proposed coal fired Gladstone Power Station. Barney Point would be an ideal place for coal storage and shipping access. Gladstone's harbor appeared an excellent resource for any expansion. Developments close to town would require environment impact studies. Best Regards/DVW.'

Doug slept until nearly 10.00 am and ate breakfast in his suite. Fresh orange juice; sliced Pawpaw fringed with blue berries. Eggs on the turn and not scrambled with ham and tomato; English muffins and coarse marmalade, one large pot of Lipton's tea. It was time to read his telegrams. The first telegram from Rachel was brief and to the point, sent from Gumption where she stayed a few days with his parents.

"I recently collided with a tall pale faced man in black as he rode an old fashioned bicycle outside 123's back door. He is the Mayor of Gumption, an active AEU Unionist you may or may not know. I've been literally, swept off my feet, his name is Alfred and we're on honeymoon at Newby Bridge."

Doug grinned and cracked "Pull the other one."

The second was from Biltong with details of the float. All the others were mainly promotional business enquiries from mining suppliers, except for Chantilly's dire missive.

'Honey, Head Office has lost contact with Wingate Lenin, Lode's African key representative in Zambia. The board has recommended that you should go there and investigate. Officially, you are now Lode's

Michael Stockdale

Overseas Business Development Executive and Overseas Operations Delegate. C&V love and kisses.'

Doug grasped the thin piece of paper, with its bland boxed in antiquated type and frowned at his 'official' company titles then slowly shook his head from side to side. His job had become a jig-saw puzzle or game of snakes and ladders, dictated by someone up top who threw the dice.

He did not expect another phone call from D'Arcy. Yet there he was on the phone and out of his mind. Shouting and weeping back at Crumpet Road because his mother was dead. Doug listened patiently to D'Arcy's hysterical outpouring:

"I'm telling yah, I stood by this scandalous shitty bed inside some shitty place where folk go to die. I watched my mother on a drip while Wally just sat there. Finally she passed away. Frail as buggery and looked like a twelve year old inside a shitty room on a shitty bed. Wally had the funds to set her up proper in a decent place: Tight as buggery,"

Then an awkward silence, as D'Arcy strove to contain his grief and recovered.

"Yah won't believe this, I've just found out my two bastard brothers carried the old lady up to a solicitor's office a month ago to change and finalize her will. I'm not to be left a penny and I've been given three days to vacate her Crumpet Road house."

Tales from Planet Gumption

"Say again?" said Doug patiently, a little bit out of his depth, but with the knowledge D'Arcy had been very fond of his mother and had lived with her for years. D'Arcy's grief then turned to anger.

"They'd carried her bodily up to the top floor of that high rise in Eagle Street to a fancy Solicitor's office where Wally's son works. Somehow they were able to get my own mother to sign a note which more or less said I was a terrible son and not entitled to anything."

"Hey, c'mon pal, get real," Doug intervened. "A blind man could see she was on prescription drugs, smoked like a chimney and drank like a skunk, but apart from that she was very old and very kind to both of us."

"Do yah know something?" D'Arcy interrupted, "I went to live and look after my mother five years ago after my sister died and I've been legally stitched up by my own family."

Doug had heard enough and concluded.

"I'll talk to you later. I've one or two things to do before I leave. I don't know much about the Law but I do have access to Lode's legal advisors. And as you're currently part-time on the payroll you may be entitled to something. Leave it with me. Take it easy. Talk to you soon."

Doug mentally visualized D'Arcy's background and personality. He had very little to go on except he was an easy go type of individual as an apprentice and fairly popular. But Doug was unable to pinpoint anything which could possibly compromise any claim towards his entitled inheritance. The same could not be said of Wally whom he had never trusted. But then who out of all three sons carried a tattoo of a heart and underneath the word 'Mother?' D'Arcy! The house in Crumpet Road had been his only home. In the literal sense D'Arcy should be entitled to something.

Broker Willy Bowery-Boyes's office was located on the second floor at 444 Queen Street and by chance was on the same floor as Queensland's Department of Mines. It occurred to Doug that the Broker was just the go-between when directly opposite behind that door there lurked a distinct possibility of something far more promising. Call it fate Doug took another punt, stepped sideways and entered its silent suite of rooms. Almost collided with late for a meeting short, rounded, affable Keppito Torres the experienced Head of Department who mistook him for somebody else.

"Good day, you must be Alec, I'm running late. Come on through to my office, I've got the Treasurer waiting."

Grabbed Doug by an arm and bustled past a series of glassed cubicles to a large substantially furnished office with a grand view of Queen Street. Seated to one side was a formally dressed man with a large open face and disappearing chin. Legs crossed. Nodded, cupped in one hand a smoldering cigarette and with a forced smile was blunt.

"Well Kep, the Cabinet was in favor of releasing some coal mining lease options, but to date we haven't found anyone interested." Then aside to Doug, "I don't think we've met? Malcolm Riddles."

Tales from Planet Gumption

"Doug Warrington," smiled Doug, "Pleased to meet you. I can honestly say I've never met anyone in this room before. I'm here just by chance and now by mistaken identity yet you mentioned coal mining options. The very thing I've been asked to follow up."

"What?" You're not Alec Sanders from Inter Pacific Exploration?" interrupted Torres.

"No, no, I'm obviously not," said Doug counting seconds and took another chance, placed his marked up copies of known resources of Queensland's coal on Torres's desk.

"But I do represent Lode International Mining and Exploration. I just happened to be on my way to Bowery-Boyes's office and changed my mind when I saw your Department of Mines sign."

"Christ, no fucking appointment, no formality?" spluttered embarrassed Torres and caught Riddle's quizzical expression who was fully aware of Lode's international reputation and nodded to Doug.

"Ok, young man, Now that you're here and as Queensland's economy is at stake and we need something solid in the pipe-line, what's your story?"

Internally, Doug's heart pounded. He paused and carefully chose his words, spoke slowly.

157

Michael Stockdale

"Initially, Lode is extremely interested in coal tenement lease options say near Oaky Creek or Newlands or at least in close proximity to Emerald. All they require are your terms."

Doug then distributed his business cards and associated Lode official literature added.

"In closing, Lode's reputation in the industry is well established overseas. It would be appreciated if you could provide an avenue or expression of interest for further discussion, ideally as soon as possible because in a few days I shall be in London. Should you have any further queries I can be contacted at Lennon's Hotel."

Doug extended one hand towards relieved Treasurer Riddles; Keppito Torres mildly elated shook hands enthusiastically and groped for words.

"Yeah, well how about that? Today we were in crisis and now it's looking good, until tomorrow then."

The entire discussion had taken less than fifteen minutes. Doug left the building with the knowledge Emerald had one sealed road which finished either end of town and like other similar towns was connected vitally by rail.

He had one more job to do before he left. Who was the best mitigation Lawyer in Lode? The Eagle Street high rise was only minutes away. He found the lift and Solicitor's office where D'Arcy's nephew Felix worked but did not enter. He had no need because there he was framed

Tales from Planet Gumption

by a wall of tinted glass. In the flesh, Wally's grotesque double in earnest deep conversation with Biltong and de Mito the dwarf Geologist a very long way from Ok Tedi, slumped in a chair. Doug sensed he had got their measure and was about to leave when he heard a manic laugh and said out aloud.

"Fuck me dead, D'Arcy Duggan in the flesh?"

He had seen enough, sidled off, caught the lift to ground floor and returned to Lennon's Hotel to send an urgent wire to Lode.

'Queensland coal lease options discussed with State Government Treasurer Malcolm Riddles and Head of Department of Mines Keppito Torres. Suggested leases were Newlands and Oaky Creek or similar. Next stop London then Zambia. Cheers, DVW.'

Early evening he received a personal call from Malcolm Riddles. He had just chaired a hastily convened meeting within his department and had spoken to Maurice Lode direct. The outcome was that letters of intent would be exchanged and agreed upon in principal and that a team of Lode finance specialists would fly immediately to Queensland.

Lode's wire was brief and said it all, 'Well done son.' Under normal circumstances Doug would have celebrated but instead turned in early. Over a very late breakfast he received hand delivered duplicates of all relevant correspondence via Torres and another call from Malcolm Riddles to drop in anytime. From a monetary point of view and again unknown to him he was now on value added percentages and entitled immediately to 3,000,000 Lode's Gold Club share issues. For a while Doug was in outer space, when his bedside phone rang.

"We have a Mr. D'Arcy Duggan and Doctor Biltong at Reception. They would like to speak with you. Shall I send them up?"

Doug placed one hand across the phone and yelled to April in the bathroom.

"Change of plan pet, we're out of here," then to Reception, "Please tell them I'm unavailable."

Grabbed his valise, his account already paid, Qantas Flight No Q428 via Sydney to London would leave in five hours. Within minutes, Flight Attendant April 'Muscles' Showers resplendent in uniform stood by his side and like Doug travelled light. Her green FJ Holden sedan parked in the hotel's car park and Doug's latest recruit temporarily hired as his personal bodyguard.

Putsi

Lenin, short but powerfully built now in his sixties, lifted his 'shades' and surveyed his next project. The area north of the farm formed part of his plan. Soon they would clear five more acres to allow for an additional light plane and erect two camouflaged portable hangers. His personal cache of weapons strategically buried in several small bunkers identified by fake gravestones. The route to and

Tales from Planet Gumption

from the Congo was always by an old sinking shaft and underground ventilation duct that terminated on the Zambian side of the border. Johannesburg's safe house already existed at Hill-Brow. Weighed down by cartridges and in need of a smoke he searched for his favorite briar with no success. Grumbled "Damn," tugged at his greying Van Dyke beard and strode impatiently back to the farmhouse. At a distance he appeared deceptively an almost comical figure pot-bellied bowed legged, dressed in absurd narrow belted denims. The 'retired' mercenary had just settled down, purchased an old farm just outside of 'Muf and married the girl found in every man's dreams. Lola La Monde Ph.D. (Guerilla Warfare) an ex-Paris Lido stripper; spoke several languages fluently.

Saddled with just one more gig for old time's sake Lenin smiled when he found and retrieved his precious tobacco and Petersen pipe. Stuffed the briar with fine Virginia lit up, sat down and brooded. His Rhodesian urologist had been almost detached in his diagnosis.

"Your prostrate is hard and cancerous. My guess is that you have until September."

Lenin's lifestyle had finally caught up with him. In and out of character he stuffed his pipe into his rear pocket hummed, 'Ten green bottles.' Tenderly returned the oldest weapon he owned into its scarred leather case. An English single barrel shotgun handmade in Kendal nicely balanced fully choked and the ideal weapon at short range. In the distance, Lola's voice mimicked Peggy Lee as she bathed in her ritual bubble bath. Rex their huge Alsatian dog snoozed across his boots. Insects danced in the early morning sun as overhead, avocado trees laden with fruit groaned and rustled in the breeze. Suddenly and from inside the house Lola screamed.

"My bath has moved!"

"What? Ach man, that's impossible," laughed Lenin.

"This is not a joke. My bath has moved, please come NOW and help."

Lenin leapt from his old wooden rocking chair and ran through the farmhouse. Lola, her face ashen surrounded by pink bubbles gripped both sides of the imported claw footed pink enameled cast iron bath. Gently plucked his beloved out, cooed "Shush now," kissed her forehead and carried her with comparative ease through to the bedroom. Around the bath was coiled a very large python, he killed professionally. Disengaged its coils and spread it out full length on the bare boards of the front porch. It was the biggest python he had ever seen just short of twenty five feet and would soon skin.

Meanwhile in the Antipodes it was eight p.m. Binned empty XXXX beer bottles embraced and rang out like church bells over Brisbane's western suburbs. The sudden silence; somewhere Dad lit up in bed and exhaled while Mum cuddled up with a romantic novel. The curious name of Tooth, the respected Dentist Doug had briefly visited and backed off: Crumpet Road's female population in its entirety prepared for bed in floral Myer dressing gowns and netted Woolworth curlers. Closed their eyes, imagined last cursory strolls through their thirty two perch manicured gardens. Brisbane's City Square was deserted long before

Tales from Planet Gumption

Doug and April flew out of Sydney bound for London.

Chantilly's request to drop everything and fly to Zambia had been difficult to fathom. Doug's knowledge of Africa was remarkably thin and forced a visit to Queensland's State Public Library where his findings had been less than favorable. Africa was plagued by revolutions or mad dictators. Two of Zambia's borders adjoined two countries, Rhodesia and the Congo, both suffered from social upheaval. The overall area had been defined as politically unstable. Doug had toyed with two well-thumbed English newspapers, The Telegraph and Times where the latter painted an appalling picture of Zambia's economic future. Kaunda its leader apparently gave goats away to solve a food crisis and was dependent on free handouts from countries that included Australia. Yet in the financial section of both newspapers he had found a brief but significant article.

'Australian mining entrepreneur's chartered plane missing over the Congo. Those on board included four prominent Australian mining identities and former Congo mercenary General Wingate Lenin.'

Why send him, when Lode employed an entire division of skilled business management specialists? Perhaps it was too close to Maurice 'Mother' Lode's activities or that the Old Man trusted Doug's infiltration methods. Whatever the reason Doug set his plan into motion; scoured speculative advertisements and government announcements. Checked out African appointments primarily and located two large exotic advertisements littered with flowery promises and Gung ho proposals.

Michael Stockdale

'Brand new house, garden and furniture, return airfares from point of recruitment. 15,000 kwachas tax paid after completion of a three year contract.'

Slammed by Fleet Street in one typical negative article 'Out of work, down and out, nowhere to go?' went so far to state that Zambia's London based recruitment office preyed openly and targeted depressed Britain's northern regions at UK Labor Exchanges. The reporter's final word was, 'Expect the worst and they could handle it.' To Doug the whole damn thing had sounded like familiar territory.

In between his Queensland forays and before he left for overseas Doug had acquired a yearning to buy something special, the ultimate tangible OZ souvenir. Boomerangs and stuffed Koala's were a plenty. Rabbit skin hats were very popular but did not really fit the bill. He had been taken by whimsy Brisbane, pottered about and caught an occasional bus or tram to anywhere. But always found himself back in sleepy Blue Hills, its overgrown hedges and so much land free of houses. He looked at properties for sale outside one or two Real Estate offices, but houses were not quite as cheap as expected. He must have had the air of a potential buyer because soon he was inside a salesman's car: On the lookout for lots of land perhaps a workers cottage maybe a creek. Doug knew it as soon as he entered the peace and rustic charm of overgrown McDonald Parade. Two years empty, a deceased estate, all forlorn, in need of paint, three blocks of land. Half an acre five minutes from the City, he purchased on the spot and bought his own little bit of Australia. Hired local Solicitors Crapper and Sons to complete the transaction and left all documentation and keys with his ANZ City Bank.

Tales from Planet Gumption

Qantas Flight Attendant April Showers was en route back to Australia by the time Doug arrived outside the quaint but reliable London Regent Street Hotel. The Midland Bank still existed as did Austin Reed. He already knew Rachel's Kensington flat had been contracted out to an Abu Dhabi letting agency. Her new address and wedding present from new husband Alfred was now a Roadman's cottage in picturesque Hades a few miles south of Burlington in the Furness district. Union strikes were still common in Britain, sterling was down and raging inflation had hit the High Street. The latter he read in the Daily Mirror and saw in the grim faces of passersby. But the sun always seemed to shine in London.

That night Doug slept well no obvious signs of jetlag. Next day refreshed, he shaved and chatted to his reflection winked one eye murmured.

"Do you have a plan my son? Aye! We'll join the Foreign Legion and play them at their own game. So you're going to go and do it? Yes, I am."

Here, Doug tapped the mirror with his razor, checked out his teeth.

"This afternoon I have an appointment with a twang a twang Major Dancer, RST and bar. My African cover at two thirty, hide your wallet Sunshine."

There was no Royal Stationary Technical room with a view when Doug entered reception precisely at two thirty. Posters adorned each wall like Gumption's Travel Agency. Now on show but in Happy Valley not in Africa, got around on skis and smiled at cameras. Doug was not disappointed by Major Theobald Thomas's entrance. Red bow tie, yellow waistcoat, trimmed moustache, sharp dog tooth suit, large gap between two prominent front teeth gushed openly and nearly carried him into his garish office.

"Please take a chair. Ah, yes I have your application and testimonials, qualifications cough, yes. I see you are married with one child who will join you later?"

Flashed the Hungarian garnet clusters on his shirt cuffs.

"You'd be entitled to a furnished house, and substantial settling in allowance. Of course you will be required to take a private medical examination, x-rays and all jabs to our cost."

Here, the rosy future of all applicants was driven by the dapper number's man twang a twang Chap, not so subtle dismissive manner who would sell his grandmother for half a farthing. His offer which just and so made the bottom line was accepted in principle but subject to a medical examination.

Signed up, a glass of sherry from the flamboyant red bow tie yellow waist-coated specialist. In the wings another English wino, RST's seedy but well-meaning Insurance expert, another sherry; make it two.

"Why not take out an expensive family life insurance policy just in case?" he declined.

Ten days later Doug climbed aboard Alitalia Flight Z209. Flew via Rome to Lusaka then transferred to Flight N23 to N'Dola. Here chaos ruled and he joined a singing, drum and whistle group of colorfully dressed pilgrims in the queue. Inside the cockpit sat their vociferous pilot engulfed by an old fashioned leather helmet and thick black beard high as a kite or drunk. Called out in Italian, Hindi, Swahili then in pock marked English, swore and blasphemed as they trooped one by one on board. No flighty stewardess. Every second passenger carried a precious 1920's Singer black sewing machine; ragged bundles few if any suitcases. The added weight from the mountain of cast-iron Singer sewing machines ignited the pilot's scripted WTF expletive riddled vocabulary. With pointed finger he insisted they should stack their sewing machines on a flimsy canvas rack adjacent to the still open hatch. Then almost childlike revved both engines manically as if in a hot-rod from a standing start. All passengers terrified. Stiff backed numb closed their eyes begged forgiveness.

Seat belts checked and fastened, the relic jerked and rattled over the runway. The hatch alongside the cockpit remained open. The plane's undercarriage moaned and shook violently. Its wheels refused to lift.

"Fuck you useless pack of fuckwit wheels," screamed the pilot whose accent had switched to transatlantic.

Pushed the relic aloft skywards, sang deep baritone over the intercom "Come flyyyyyyyy with me toooooo N'Dola," turned sharply starboard then dived towards the runway. Unsecured, the rack's contents changed to home grown Singer bombs, fell through the open hatch and splattered the runway. The multi-national stamped his authority with a scant reminder.

"Read the fucking manual. Any complaints and I'll drop you motherfuckers off just the same."

But nobody said a word, rolled their eyes; worshipped idols.

The pilot's silent majority delivered intact at N'Dola Airport and at night. Inside, Mine Personnel's Stefan Bemba waited patiently, immaculately dressed down to his patent leather shoes, smart dinner suit late for an important Government function. In one hand he held aloft a large white card with Doug's name printed boldly. Doug approached from the rear and crudely introduced himself.

"Hey-up pal, that's me."

"Ah, is it Mr. Warrington? Did you have a pleasant trip?"

Stefan flashed white teeth and smiled down at Doug's crumpled attire. Introduced himself formally

"My name is Stefan, and I shall be escorting you to Mufulira."

Doug grimaced, taken aback by the black lad's posh accent and decent strides. Impressed by the easy way he had commandeered his valise and guided him to his spotlessly clean blue Peugeot. Once seated, dictated politely in Oxford English, "Please fasten safety belt," then accelerated from a standing start until the vehicle reached 90mph. Doug froze, paralyzed said nothing. Stefan drove like a madman down an unlit road, past numerous but unseen native compounds, packed village pubs shrouded by thick charcoal smoke without any hesitation. Totally unconcerned lived dangerously, swept through Central Africa's black impenetrable night like a guillotine and dramatically, screeched to a halt outside RST's Mufulira transit house.

"Hey-up," said Doug and climbed out shaken, "Thanks a lot Stefan. Enjoy the Do. Ten to one you speak French and read Latin?"

"Of course, my pleasure, you'll find something to eat inside, Amos will make tea or coffee. "Welcome to Mufulira."

Spun the wheels as Doug watched on and vanished. It was the black of night and in the distance, the throb of native drums spread like treacle.

Dawn: The omnipresent odor from burning charcoal. High pitched long conversations from passing natives. Louder softer raised their voices long after they passed each other. Doug's first impression of Mufulira was fair to middling it appeared to be a presentable modern European town with most facilities. Staff lived in concrete detached houses. Seniority determined the size of house. All had large gardens, and were located in tree lined streets with sealed roads. At the rear of each house sat the servants' quarters about the size of one small single bedroom. Doug's allocated house was at the bottom of Omelo Avenue, three hundred yards from an unfenced Congo border. His Mine settling-in allowance subsidy vanished immediately, substituted by RST's rental fee for house furnishings and a huge variety of keys. Doug's next official stop on his guided tour would be Chibuluma approximately twenty miles away.

Chibuluma's copycat landscaped European town was encased by a high security fence where Doug would work in RST's satellite Engineering Office and travel to each day, six days per week. Usually, by Company bus to and from Mufulira. To drive alone was discouraged by the Company. Those who chose to travel solo were urged to travel by convoy in case of attack by Congolese rebels. Brief, matter of fact circulated memorandums were a daily event, 'Acts of violence were on the increase.' Two weeks in; the local native run garage where Doug first saw the bowser man shave his face with a strand of wire was blown up. Three weeks in sotto voice Security advised a crowd of new recruits.

"Should you accidentally hit a pedestrian on the road; don't stop. You will be stoned to death by angry villagers."

Doug had not really adjusted to this new 'risky business' lifestyle and besides he had yet to hear from Lenin. The joint was without a doubt, action packed 24/7 and he wondered if he was up to it. During his first few weeks the Brits he encountered rode the waves with jokes or put-downs and took the piss out of everything. Most had been out of work in the UK, one or two were there to pitch against South Africa's Apartheid. But the majority appeared to be on the make. The most popular racket accessed by the Asian businessmen was the expatriate overseas cash transfer ceiling. Two thousand kwachas transferred to any British Bank generated four hundred kwachas in the hand. This method of easy cash applied because most expatriates expected a large tax free incentive bonus on completion of their contract.

Doug's role in Chibuluma was of no significance. He was just another recruit which paid commission. Nobody appeared to be under pressure to meet deadlines or did much work at all. The only competition was between Heads of Departments who affected lifestyles reminiscent of the 'British Raj:' Tiffin, silver teapots with all the trimmings. Planned holidays in Switzerland and took their surroundings for granted like errant windbags without substance. Rumor had it RST's status had changed to that of Consultant, financed by the Government from overseas donations. It appeared to be yet another racket, more jobs for Zambian Public Servants and big commissions for off-shore Agencies.

Socially Chibuluma's parties were extravagant, subsidized by a failing monetary system where projects always ran over budget. No one cared in isolated Chibuluma. As for Doug, he relied on the company of some Welsh con artist expats who worked in Mufulira and socialized at Mufulira's Public swimming pool. Not far from Omelo Avenue but preceded by a long ritual key locking procedure; all internal and external access doors; simple kitchen cupboards, laundry, pantry, bedroom wardrobes and all iron-barred windows progressively through to the front iron barred security door. His garden's front gates were heavily chained and padlocked. This tedious procedure was standard practice and it was recommended to return home before dusk.

Michael Stockdale

Doug had anticipated his assignment would be brief if not premature after reading about bilharzia (sleeping sickness) that lurked in still languid pools of water and about the dreaded eggs from the Putsi fly which were lethal. These flies produced invasive tiny worms which penetrated the skin, fed and multiplied with crippling results. Doug was very glad he was not married and lumbered with kids. His excuse when asked was that his 'wife' had entered hospital and was unable to travel.

His daily journey by Company bus was a bonus, lightened up by new fellow travelers from England's northern depressed areas. They had arrived penniless, no money in their pockets underfed pale and bedraggled with massive chips on their shoulders sometimes with large families. Newcastle Joe was one of them employed as a Welder who did a runner.

"Another house for sale Hinny?" queried Fred from Shield's.

"Aye, yon canny Joe's sold his rented Mine house to an Asian lad at bargain price. And sold all his rented furniture to his pal," said Ron from Bradford

"Not Joe the Geordie we'd befriended when we arrived?" asked Paddy deep in debt.

"The very one" said Piker Petersen with a lisp. "I bought his car off him yesterday and I'll pick it up today."

But unknown to them, Newcastle born and bred Joe had said early adios goodbye, and sold it twice to yet to another pal he knew because he trusted him.

It may have been on a Sunday when the sound of rapid gun fire found Doug wide eyed glued behind a tree at 15 Omelo Avenue. Beyond his garden fence he counted and watched over a hundred terror stricken people, men women and children, crash through the undergrowth from the Congo border. Pursued by men with guns; reportedly later rounded up interned then shot. The same day Fidelis, his mandatory cleaner and gardener cleared off to Lusaka with his family.

It seemed apt that after a couple of days still in panic mode Doug felt woozy at work and called into Chibuluma's hospital. The Bradford born English Doctor was very young his brand new stethoscope tagged in white ink. Checked Doug's pulse, tapped his joints, thrust a thermometer into his mouth, commented on the remarkable weather and finalized.

"Cheers pal, and no, I've never been to Gumption. Try these."

It was a packet of white tablets given with the proviso if they did not work to call back in a couple of days. The discharged patient vaguely cheered up returned to a packed Reception audience in happy mode, entertained by a large white enamel bowl perched precariously on the desk. Probationer Annie Lobeto on her first professional assignment proudly circulated and showed off its contents, an estimated only ten minutes old four hundred white ecstatic worms removed from a young woman's stomach. Doug vomited.

Michael Stockdale

The revered Chief Engineer of RST's satellite engineering office picked at the selection of nuts, topped up his English breakfast tea, placed his Motor magazine to one side waved agreeably in Doug's direction and told him to go home. Rest and stay in bed. Dismissed and excused they dropped him off at Omelo Avenue. Portly, officious his replacement cleaner Miriam, watched as he staggered, bogeyed feverish across the lounge and collapsed on the bed. She did not move. Doug shouted and fought demons then blacked out. There was no more movement, just an empty silence. Superstitious wide-eyed Miriam stood at a distance in the lounge. Crossed her chest and panicked. Strode outside and yelled out to next door's House Girl.

"Mr. Doug is dying. Fetch the Doctor."

Walked, quit her job immediately and cleared off before he arrived. Hospitalized, Doug fought strange imaginary battles but recovered, summed up by the Hospital's Physician.

"You'll be fine son, incidents like this come with the job."

Doug's incarceration plus Lenin's no show modified his plans when he met South African Lola. Someone he had chatted up in the local Supermarket and debated the benefits of English chutney. Said she was an ex-dancer by trade and could speak several languages. She had attended Taffy's the skilled metallurgist part-time con-artist's parties occasionally. Intrepid Taffy had already sold top mechanic Doug an overpriced Jeep, played Poker for real money and on the night arm in arm with Doug, tempted smooth attractive Lola to join the fray; she who coolly won the Pot and wisely walked away. The Pot contained US$800.00 or about the same amount Doug paid for the Jeep. Lola had evened up the score and suggested that they should spend the cash on a short Victoria Falls vacation. Why not? Doug was going to skid-addle anyway, better now than later. So it was that Doug and Lola hit the road to Victoria Falls.

Night and straight ahead the silhouettes of two gigantic hippos about to take an evening dip; ignored their tooting horn. Waddled on at leisurely pace then abruptly waddled off out of sight to an undisclosed destination. Doug pricked his ears convinced there was something else out there. Something that sounded like thunder or similar to the crowd's response at Gumption's Craven Park when Castle scored or witnessed the fourth Hewson interception. Imagine then that the thunder increased binomially, with a seething, writhing jungle as background. Something outside made a God awful racket as they approached Victoria Falls.

Louder and louder almost deafening, it beggared Doug's belief with its size and sheer majesty. A huge swirling cauldron created by nature. Steep unfenced cliffs clouded by mile high spray made humans look like ants. Initially Doug was reluctant to camp beside a vast molten ice-age vat of untamed water. Magnificent yes, but overwhelmingly scary and something he would never forget. It was raw and had no protective barriers to prevent anyone from falling into the chasm. Nothing to prevent their precious Jeep assumed to be safely parked slowly inch towards the precipitous edge. Minus its disintegrated hand brake mechanism, Lola fortunately spotted just in time.

Michael Stockdale

She had already booked two separate grass huts said she was Catholic. Then after a little red wine and bratwurst confided blandly she was happily married to madman, mercenary and hired killer called Wingate Lenin. But not to worry because he knew where she was and relied on her to act as Doug's interim contact.

"What? Wingate bloody Lenin?" cried Doug.

Choked on his fresh coconut, full of olives and sweet potato garnished with parsley; perhaps a little more English mustard: Fresh rye bread, lashings of home-made English chutney. Spat out the olive pips, nearly broke a tooth. Belched and spluttered.

"That's the very man I'm here to see. You're not having me on?"

Lola grinned at Doug's red face and confided.

"It was Winnie's idea to pick you up in the Supermarket. He'd some unfinished business in the Congo. That's why we'd always meet in the Supermarket. Sometimes Taffy went on assignments with him and on the last occasion to view a proposition. The Jeep deal, failed poker games and Taffy's social activities are part of our cover. It's highly likely there'll be more social unrest and your movements in Zambia will be restricted. We're used to it but plan to get you over the Zambian border very soon. In the meantime enjoy your visit to our country. Be prepared. Military action will intensify and don't invest in Zambia's currency soon it'll be worthless."

Tales from Planet Gumption

Doug had never heard so much tripe in his life. But had he not been in Africa he had to believe it. That night he farted many times and slept fitfully.

Next day found Doug circumspect; resigned to expect anything. Trapped by circumstances beyond his control he questioned his sanity still unable to accept Lola's hackneyed explanations. According to her, Lenin was alive and well so why had Lode sent him to darkest Africa? It did not make sense. He would have to wait to find out. Meanwhile Lola seemed intent to round off their trip and visit Wanki's Game Reserve before returning to Mufulira. The man from No 123 brushed aside his negative thoughts and decided to go along with the perceived charade.

Showered, scrubbed up and fed, Lola took the wheel and entered the Wanki Game Reserve without a guide, they did not need one. She knew the way and intuitively pushed the Jeep undeterred through dense three story high eye-piercing grass. Back in the real world tourist Doug froze at the sight of several towering curious Giraffes. Their enormous heads, huge vacant eyes hovered low against the vehicle's windscreen. Then ignored, casually dismissed them as mere humans and wandered off. Lola squealed with delight drove on slowly until they came across a large picnic area. In the distance and as far as the eye could see the never ending veldt. Then out of nowhere stepped a native in khaki uniform Lola spoke to in dialect and he advised a big bull elephant was in the area. Translated

"Him take daily swim in nearby water hole, him ass hole, him monster."

Michael Stockdale

Lola eased the Jeep down a beaten track. Then stopped; one hundred yards ahead the destined water hole surrounded by a shallow clearing. Close to the water's edge a white VW Kombi in reverse packed with Nuns in full regalia. The Nuns stood upright in the vehicle and urged the driver to reverse closer to the water hole perimeter. Excited, by vague tremulous movements of the water; tiny rivulets that expanded slowly into larger waves as the Bull Elephant's head gradually surfaced. Its eyes initially curious quickly objected to the intrusion and rose up swiftly, waved its massive trunk with anger. Tossed its long tusks in their direction and emerged in total. His Majesty the gigantic Bull Elephant was not amused bristled with contempt. Unable to reverse the driver panicked, the Kombi stalled. The passengers screamed clutched each other and their rosaries. The mammoth limbered up within twenty feet. Flapped his ears, raised his trunk prepared to charge. The Kombi's engine fired, bogged rear wheels slipped and spun. The elephant charged the moment the Kombi's wheels hit terra firma. Rome had smiled down. The frustrated challenger watched as the Holy Kombi vanished. Irked, he tossed his trunk again and peered in the direction of the Jeep. Nobody moved; Doug and Lola transfixed. The elephant thrust his body in all directions ripped at minor saplings, bellowed a further challenge with no response flapped his ears turned and grumbled. Grumbled like an old man; walked slowly away in the opposite direction.

Lenin's planned diversion before his next Congo trip had been to blow up the local Explosives Factory but someone beat him to it. Above the decimated plant a huge black cloud hovered indefinitely and when Doug arrived back at Omelo Avenue Miriam's replacement had cleared off. Externally, his house appeared unaffected but internally ceilings of the lounge and kitchen covered the floors. Within hours, the military occupied Mufulira's streets. Armored vehicles cruised down Omelo Avenue, rotated gun turrets and aimed at every house. Armed foot soldiers stood inside every Bank while others took up positions outside schools and shops. Overhead and usually early evening low flying foreign Jet fighters deafened and intimidated residents. Unconcerned uniformed implacable Chinese joined shoppers. Drastic supermarket food shortages fed speculation. Within days access out of Zambia suddenly ceased, all borders were officially closed. Externalization of cash was prohibited and there was nothing anyone could do about it. The value of Zambian currency dived, promised bonuses withered in Zambian Banks. Something was going on. But what Doug had no idea, unless of course it was another diversion.

These thoughts went through Doug's head as he walked up Omelo Avenue's driveway after dusk. He had had it with these mandatory servants who always cleared off after a bit of action. Right then he fancied a bacon sandwich when there was a heavy knock on his front door. Doug faltered, nearly dropped the fry-pan and approached his unexpected visitor with considerable trepidation. Switched on the outside light but did not recognize the man.

"My name is Lenin, I believe I am expected?"

Doug gawped as the bearded much older man swept past him then strolled both hands clasped behind his back to and fro across the lounge before he spoke.

"You know why we are both here?"

"Your whereabouts pal? The official drum was that you went missing in a Congo plane crash. Lode sent me to investigate. I read about the crash in the newspapers."

"Missing? Shit, *I am* your contact. I was never on the plane."

Lenin grimaced, quickly realized he was dealing with an idiot and studied Doug's confused expression.

"Ach man, no matter,"

Pulled out a small canvas bag concealed in his shirt pocket and placed part of its contents into one hand.

"These are what we in the trade call industrial diamonds, used in specialized machine tools and other machinery and not those found at Breakfast at Tiffany's. It's really about feeding the western industrial world. You were elected as Courier for these diamonds by Lode."

"Hang-on pal," said Doug, "Why me, why not you? Nobody has mentioned this in dispatches," shook his head in disbelief.

Lenin sat down on the Company settee and laughed out aloud continued,

"I am a wanted man in several countries. This house is where all our couriers stay when in town. It's a fixed arrangement with an element inside Personnel. Your servant's abode at the rear of the garden has an additional false removable wall. Behind it is an access to a ladder and ventilation tunnel below. That tunnel runs 100 meters beneath the Congo border and terminates at a disused sinking headgear and service shaft. We use it to obtain diamonds in exchange for arms."

Doug wavered, never in his entire life had he met such a candid man. In the matter of twenty minutes he warmed to Lenin's concise and rapid explanations. There was no fat glib reaction at his reluctance to accept the diamonds. Lenin had shrugged it off and now appeared more concerned with his safety. Doug nodded in agreement and said nothing. Lenin enjoyed the pantomime, took an explanatory breather.

"Initially Plan A, meant we were going to fly you out but with all this activity in the sky we have adopted Plan B which never fails. By the way the border between Zambia and Rhodesia has been closed indefinitely. Right now you would be unable to leave conventionally by road or plane."

"So I'm buggered if I do and I'm buggered if I don't? Is that it?"

"Ha-Ha, precisely except for one thing called theatrics which never fails. The border may be closed but on the other side is an armed division of South Africans soldiers billeted at Makuti,"

Lenin eyed Doug's condition and waited patiently; the kid was sick with God knows what and underweight.

Michael Stockdale

"We go tonight at midnight. Lock up as you usually do and throw away the keys. Travel light and bring your passport, visa. Take this it is an official Zambian leave of absent document for emergencies."

Lenin rose up, returned the canvas bag to his shirt pocket; brushed off imaginary dust. Stretched out a crisp cold muscular hand to Doug's soft palm and grasped it firmly.

"Be at your garden gate at midnight wear old clothes and serviceable boots. I'll see my own way out."

Clicked his heels, turned and vanished in much the same way he had arrived.

At precisely midnight Doug locked the padlocks on his garden gate but did not throw his keys away until he heard then saw his Jeep with Lenin behind the wheel.

"Is that my vehicle Sunshine? It looks different and sounds great."

"Ach Man, let's say I've borrowed it. Put this blacking on your face and hands. No more talking."

They sped into the night at 230km/hour or more than twice the speed of normal traffic. Imported sixteen inch wheels, all weather tires, a supercharged V8 and lowered suspension. Doug's machine had been modified within hours by Lenin's sponsored Lola-Perfume's Middle East based European racing team. Now on Safari, all expenses paid, plus commission in Mozambique. Pre-dawn, the Police helicopter hovered and tracked them for five miles outside Lusaka, then lost interest after they identified its registration and veered off. Suddenly Lenin's shortwave radio spluttered with Lola's seductive voice.

"Hello darling, good news the Zambian border will be open today for eight hours, and closed again until further notice."

This vital piece of information changed everything. There was no need for haste. Lenin spoke in Afrikaans to someone on his short wave radio and then in English to Doug.

"Ach Man, we've been lucky. I can drop you off at Mukuti if you want and then return to Zambia before they close the border. But then how would you travel through Rhodesia? Maybe your best bet is Johannesburg and Alitalia. You'll be OK if you drive through Rhodesia and head for South African Customs at Beitbridge."

Lenin continued to think out aloud.

"Look man, I'll take you as far as Makuti and drop the weapons. You take the Jeep and I'll find my own way back. Do we have a deal?"

"Aye, it sound's really good to me. What weapons?"

Lenin stifled a chuckle and ignored the question.

Michael Stockdale

Sooner than expected they neared a cleared space which stated clearly, "STOP Zambian border." But neither man could detect any activity. Curiously, the Custom's pole barrier was vertical and not horizontal. Not a single soul was in sight. Lenin forced to leave the car to search for someone in uniform to stamp their visas. Found two smiling co-operative officials sprawled drunk and half asleep in their untidy office. The obliging man stamped their visas and the runaways crossed the border elated.

Doug's old Secondary School Headmaster's favorite book was The Lions of Makuti. Half a dozen roared all around when the Jeep packed it in and overheated. "Ignore them," laughed Lenin and lit his pipe. Doug jumped out to inspect the damage, lifted the bonnet thrown by the engineering handiwork and mighty engine. Weighed up the sixteen inch wheels and lowered suspension. Thought, 'What a beauty,' when the swarm of elephant flies descended.

"Christ Almighty," went out his cry, "Jesus, Jesus I'm being eaten alive."

But lost the fight and rejoined by now hysterical Lenin who nearly swallowed his pipe from laughing. Doug groaned.

"What the fucking hell was that? It was bloody painful I can tell you. Wow! Mama Mia. That was the closest fucking thing to being eaten by cannibals."

Neither men saw the truck until then. They did not move. They could not move even if they wanted to. In the distance a large heavily manned truck approached, possibly six wheeled and camouflaged. Voices, foreign guttural accents maybe South African, several leapt to the ground as their war machine pulled over. Martial muscled artists in fatigues walked around the modified Jeep, ignored the profile of two Israeli-MX80 Mortars on the rear seat and under canvas; tapped its roof and greeted them with smiles. The officer had recognized the famous Lenin, asked for his autograph and posed for a photograph. Took control, replaced the fractured radiator hose clip and topped-up the Jeep's radiator. The Lions of Makuti roared their disapproval once again as Lenin relaxed smoked his pipe; yarned about the old days with a group of soldiers in their own language. One told him that the road would be mined south of the Zambian border within a matter of days. The soldiers finished their cigarettes, shook hands then waved them on.

Mufulira's grapevine had been up to date; South African troops operated in Rhodesia, but these would be the first Doug had ever seen. Lenin's body language and the way he had been received suggested he was very important and an authority on Zambian military activities. There was no way back, the road on which they had travelled would be heavily mined. Lenin did not appear the slightest concerned and had accepted the officer's invitation to billet at the now militarized Makuti Motel. War of a kind had been declared in milliseconds. Lenin knew the way like the back of his hand and parked the Jeep around the rear in a private driveway. Surrounded by peaceful landscaped gardens he unloaded the Israeli-MX80 Mortars, winked at the impassive soldier on sentry duty and symbolically placed them on top of an old wooden wheelbarrow full of flowers. Turned to Doug and said, "In God we trust," and grabbed him by both shoulders. Grinned like the madman he attempted to hide and failed.

"You did well you did very well not to lose your nerve. Always tell the truth, believe me it is far easier than lying. Tomorrow is another day, don't waste it."

Spun on one heel and tapped his head

"Oh and before I forget I have something for you. Wait here I have a small gift or souvenir."

Lenin strode back to the Jeep and returned with a pair of Safari boots discretely sized by Lola while at Victoria Falls. They fitted perfectly. Doug's companion, the man with a ruthless past was suddenly lost for words. He was not very good at farewells. Mumbled he would probably find his way back by parachute, shook hands turned sharply and was soon swallowed up by a small but merry contingent of former colleagues.

The man behind the Motel counter refused to accept any cash from Doug, added that he could stay the night, dinner at six, breakfast at seven, would Doug like a beer? Doug had several beers, showered and changed and almost fell asleep basking in the Motel's swimming pool. Next day scrubbed up and relaxed he thanked his Host and quickly drove through and out of elegant "Made in Britain" Salisbury. The civilized silence in its outskirts was overwhelming and contrasted markedly with that of Mufulira. The road out was partially tree lined, well-maintained and surrounded by spectacular countryside devoid of traffic. He met few

Tales from Planet Gumption

vehicles on the road and drove until late afternoon.

Then came across a slice of history, a mirage he called 'Lilliput,' an old sleepy original bush town which reminded him of Queensland, Australia. Antique rocking chairs, unpainted wooden blinds, worn timber unpainted verandas closeted sun spotted fast asleep old people who dozed collectively. Inside another time or space, quaint timber houses, ancient motorcars and Raleigh bicycles. Pot plants full of ferns, old fashioned petrol bowsers all similar to those he had seen en route to Gladstone. His Jeep's number plates attracted attention, and the same standard awkward question.

"What was really happening in Zambia?"

The owner of 'Lilliput's' only Pub decorated by torn and faded touring Band posters from another year, refused payment of any kind, instead put him up, washed and fed him. Before he departed he left an envelope with a note scrawled 'Thank you' at Reception; inside US$200.00.

It was a moving, melancholy moment when Doug left that tranquilized small bush town. More like a retirement village, its inquisitive elderly inhabitants lulled by padded rocking chairs, resigned to wait indefinitely to see what fate would offer. No real perspective or definite grasp of the inevitable wide spread of chaos which would or could follow.

The simple sign read 'Zimbabwe Ruins' seemed miles from anywhere. Here, Doug took a chance and pointed his Jeep down an uneven beaten track and came across a monument of extraordinary dimensions maybe the same age as Gumption's Abbey, a collection of massive stone structures erected in the 11th century where no mortar kept the stones together. It was far more ancient than expected. Not a soul about. He explored and walked along a narrow surface tunnel around a cone shaped building where the air was cooler than expected. The plaque said it was the heart between the horns of Africa and the focal point of ancient traders, as far away as China.

Escapees were a common sight at Beitbridge. They saw them every day. They filled in forms and answered questions. Men dressed in brown uniforms saw some value in his Jeep and forced Doug to pay a fee, but not in Zambian Kwachas. Once through Customs he relaxed and drove on but not in haste, through and over large mountain ranges, across wide plains, stopped off at Rustenburg for some fresh orange juice his destination Johannesburg.

It was festive, vocal and vibrated. It was Saturday night live 8.00pm when Doug arrived in Hill Brow, an inner Johannesburg suburb and the mood outside was as if he had landed on another planet. Beset with noisy crowded pavements, music everywhere. Lenin's safe house address lost and gone forever. He booked into one of many modern Hotels, slept deeply through Sunday and most of Monday.

Lenin's flight from Rhodesia to Mufulira was delayed by bad weather. Two days had already passed when the unmarked plane circled high above his farm at dusk as he prepared to jump. "At the count of three, good luck," yelled the pilot and Lenin leapt into space. Felt the mild resistance of the parachute, the thrill of being airborne and almost home. Jostled by a western wind and from where he glided earthbound all the farm lights appeared to be on. His downward descent crisp and clean; accurately positioned to land three hundred yards south of his cache of weapons pre-empted in case of unwanted visitors. His first thoughts were of Lola now safe in Zurich, Switzerland. She would stay with her sister while he was away. For a dying man he landed strongly and quickly removed the parachute. Rolled methodically and deposited inside an empty twenty gallon drum placed there for such emergencies.

Lenin flinched when he saw and counted the collection of ramshackled vehicles strewn outside his gabled front door. His visitors had to be Congolese insurgents and he estimated even without seeing them he would have to deal with between twenty and thirty armed men. On the farm's porch he picked out the tall ungainly outline of an armed, loudly dressed black man smoking and caught the strong whiff of Dacca. The driveway was booby-trapped for such emergencies. He covered his face and any other exposed flesh with blacking. Selected his weapons carefully, two Israeli mortars to finish off stragglers. Activated the booby-trapped driveway, then positioned and aimed the two mortars at less than seventy yards away from the farmhouse entrance. On top of the farm's roof was an incendiary device that could be activated by a small radio device; if still alive he could always build another farm.

Concealed conventional and insulated 8 mm battery operated movie cameras were located in various points throughout the farm house and connected to a screen inside his two man concrete bunker. The fake grave stone above it said Charles Dickens. All were operated by remote control. He activated each camera individually. The lounge camera picked out Taffy the metallurgist dressed in black overalls and white bandanna who issued orders to that two faced short shit assassin part-time Zam-Am Pilot Dave de Mito. Both carried automatic rifles and Army issue revolvers. Other cameras revealed at least fifteen armed Congolese grouped inside the kitchen, several more dispersed in all three bedrooms. Ultimately, behind each window lurked a gun.

Lenin made the decision and detonated the incendiary in his bitumen tarred farm house roof. Simultaneously, rapid fire flashed from windows then ceased the moment molten tar penetrated and fell through ceilings. Lenin pulled the mortar's pre-tensioned wires as the panicked rebels spilled towards the porch and attempted to vacate the raging inferno. The shrapnel cut an instant swathe and felled the remaining farmhouse structure. Those who attempted to flee in different directions he picked off one by one with his scoped night-sight high powered rifle. Meanwhile the bush to the north dry as tinder caught on fire and raced half a mile in seconds.

Only two men emerged left standing; Taffy and Dave de Mito. Each waved a flag of truce, something white attached to their guns. They called out, "We come as friends," placed their weapons on the ground and edged towards an ex-Army Land Rover. Lenin paused and watched them climb aboard and start the engine nodded his head whispered, "Thank you," and detonated the driveway's mines. 'Kerplommm,' the Land Rover and other vehicles instantly transformed to twisted shimmering metal sailed skywards then somersaulted or exploded. Lenin walked slowly back to his bunker, scratched his crutch said, "God is good," and crossed himself.

Several days had passed since Doug had arrived in Johannesburg and this Sunday morning he parked in one of the City's inner leafy streets. Tremors from mining detonations deep underground filtered throughout the vehicle. Not far away a group of native South Africans argued on the pavement. One, a woman broke away and ran in his direction chased by another woman. The first woman slipped and fell. Her assailant paused and picked up a rock. Straddled her victim's chest and smashed her skull until she was dead. Doug remained frozen inside the Jeep. He had just witnessed his first hand to hand brutal murder by a woman. Church bells rang as he slowly reversed and drove back to his hotel. His eventual departure gauged around his full recovery from the Zambian episode. Mentally, this single incident chewed at his confidence.

In the silence of his suite he pondered about his future. The word Rutile, came to mind? Union Corporation's Head office was in town and they had an interest in Queensland's Consolidated Minerals sand mining outfit. Sometimes he imagined old Lenin seated comfortably on his shoulder one eye open armed to the hilt.

"Ach man, give them a call."

Their office was in Marshall Street and only a short leisurely walk from his hotel. He gave them a call and made an appointment with their Engineering Division because they always knew at least two years ahead which side of the bread was buttered.

Michael Stockdale

Gordon Dean, Union's Chief Designer had come over as genial yet circumspect on the phone and an appointment was made for 10.30 a.m. the following day. Marshall Street contained many large solid impressive old buildings and considerable traffic manned enterprisingly by University Students during morning peak hours. Union Corporation's Mining House building too, was impressive and policed by quietly spoken aged tall stooped suited retainers adorned with military medals. No one was allowed to proceed without confirmation. One guided Doug to the visitors' recess; iced water, club leather furniture, veneered wooden walls and traditional old oil paintings of the veldt.

Ten minutes later he was directed personally to the lift with instructions.

"Mr. Dean the Chief Designer will see you in his office."

Knock, knock, a Cockney voice rasped "Come," and he entered. Dean's office was spacious and uncluttered. He did not rise from his seat or extend his hand. He wore no jacket was gruff middle-aged, white haired and perhaps short in the leg. His sharp blue eyes, magnified by thick lensed horned-rim glasses inspected and assessed Doug's appearance. When Dean finally elected to speak his accent had changed to south of the Thames as he gave a brief summary about the company's activities. Then cut short and asked to see some of Doug's credentials. Said he was not concerned with qualifications or background muttered, "…more often fake inside the trade." Doug passed his card over Dean's desk and apologized for not doing it sooner. Dean grimaced, read the fine print suddenly interested.

Tales from Planet Gumption

"You said on the phone you had just arrived from Zambia and are passing through? Tell me more about yourself and who you represent without this bull-shit," and slid Doug's calling card back across the desk.

Doug had no hidden agenda and had tired of Dean's idle banter. Rose to his feet; retaliated.

"Don't patronize me. I came here with good intention by pure default and circumstance. I've been shot at and nearly died in your God damn Africa just doing my job and in the last quarter of an hour you've treated me like a piece of shit. I'm here in your office on business with a serious proposition. We've got the possibility of kick starting a twenty million dollar sand mining project that may or may not use Union's sand-mining technology. I've wasted my time. Fuck you Sunshine, I'm out of here."

"Stop right there," cried Dean

Reared up from his desk both arms askew, grinned and asked if Doug preferred coffee or tea, said his name was Gordon chuckled grabbed and shook him by the hand.

"That was fucking awesome. You can use the office next door and I'll line up some people to meet."

Lenin vanished off Doug's left shoulder. Doug decided to bugger off instead and leave Dean to it. Wrote on his desk blotting pad his immediate needs and left. Returned briefly and shouted.

Michael Stockdale

"Hey Gordon, thanks a lot, I'll give you a bell sometime tomorrow."

At first sight Johannesburg appeared as a thriving prosperous bustling city when compared to depressed Britain's high unemployment and raging inflation. Yet underneath its colorful canopy it harbored a large military occupation on call twenty-four hours. Similarly and as seen, the misleading gloss of modern architecture in Zambia created a false cozy picture of prosperity when in actual fact the country was broke. As for politically embattled embargoed Rhodesia the writing was definitely on the wall. Yet on the day Doug walked down Joubert Street almost everything was obtainable and affordable.

But the violence witnessed was apparently common and untenable. Popular targets were ordinary housewives who dropped their husbands off to work. Targeted at traffic lights or when stationary and if all doors were not locked. Elderly white people who lived in flats accessed by public lifts appeared the most vulnerable; their spines slashed by razors inside the lift then robbed.

Still in Joubert Street Doug paused absent mindedly outside a small café and in the reflection of its window saw a familiar Gumption face and thought he was dreaming.

"Good God Almighty, Huric Errol."

It was the man from Laramie highly intelligent, slow talking and passionate. The son of a Preston based butcher, the brother of the Pie

Tales from Planet Gumption

Lady's lover Flynn Archibald Errol. Best man at Sugar Ray Robinson's wedding, the master of ceremonies at the wedding reception held at The King's Head Pub, Broughton-in-Furness.

"Hey Huric," cried Doug. "How yah doing?

"Well, well if isn't Douglas V for Victor, I was just saying to our Alma the other day. I wonder what Douglas V for Victor is up to these days?"

"You lying cheeky bastard, pull the other one."

"No seriously, how are you old son? You look fit and well, like the boots but by the looks of things you can't be doing very well."

Then together said, "That's the same bloody coat you left town in," and hooted with laughter until their sides hurt.

"Hey," said Huric, "We're having a christening after party at our house in Mondo Kane, this Saturday night and it'll be easy to find because we've installed a mini-shipyard hooter and two large Chinese beacons. Hey, hey! It's our sixth kid and everyone there will be from Gumption. The Salthouse Wiggles fresh back from Australia, the Pickles family, missus and three kids from Ormsgill, King George and his personal dragon. The Vicar of Dimbleby after the christening. We're supplying all the food and drink. So get yourself there this Saturday night. Here's my card with details."

Michael Stockdale

"Sounds great to me," said Doug. "We'll see you then. Take it easy." Both men parted and walked in opposite directions.

Doug's Zambian soiree had its limitations. His body had taken a hammering. Mentally fatigued but elated with the day's proceedings he headed back to his hotel totally knackered. Stayed in and out of bed for most of Thursday and Friday, ate all meals in his suite. Messages from Dean lay by his bed untouched. He had taken the rest of the week off and there was no South African television to watch.

Hello Saturday opened with a bowl of fruit. Mondo Kane was an outer suburb just under an hour away by car according to Reception. At 6.00pm he showered and prepared for Huric's party. Purchased a magnificent bouquet of flowers and large box of Swiss chocolates, two bottles of fine South African Shiraz and hired one of the hotel's chauffeur-driven limousines for the entire evening. Dressed casually; smart russet single breasted corduroy jacket, cavalry twill trousers, white shirt and his everyday footwear. Lenin's gift from the Gods, his boots with the snake skin insert. Zipped molded rubber sprung Cuban heels and wafer thin soles; the finest imported Italian leather.

Two large Chinese Beacons led the way to a detached bungalow on half an acre. It appeared to be an upmarket suburb judging by the number of expensive European vehicles parked. Large blocks of manicured lawns garlanded by ornamental bushes and the occasional spread of giant Jacaranda trees. Security gates and subsequent high wired fences, the overall impression was one of guarded substance and wealth. Joseph the Hotel driver for the night spoke to the device in one of the gate's columns and the gates silently swung open. But as Doug climbed out of the car it looked and sounded as though half of Gumption had been invited. Huric's voice rang out from the front veranda.

"Hey-up, it's our Douglas, come over here and say hello to my mother. Hey you lot, here's someone all the way from 123 Lord Street that may or may not be famous."

Huric's after-christening party now doubled as a welcome for his mother who was there on six weeks holiday. Doug knew this territory very well but was not too sure who would be the first to start a fight, the women or the men? Huric's mother's face was typically Gumption, broad and pan-faced, overly friendly. Confident Mabel linked his arm and guided him into the crowd of revelers, now a widow and fancy free enquired, "Beer or spirits?" Some of the men around the bar he recognized by their body language, the same old rigmarole. Mabel pulled out a Polaroid camera and told Doug to go and stand with them. An instant picture said it all. Three he recognized as from the Alfs or was it from somewhere else? The man in the middle was him, grim faced, squinty eyed and unsmiling he hardly recognized.

His life over the past few years had left its mark. He did not like it. Where was the lad he used to know, the one that not so long ago cracked jokes with pals in Kelly's Music Shop doorway? Teased the girls behind the counter in Woolworths, cajoled Frank Woods for a discount on a new tie?

The photograph and past sentiments stirred his loins. This Mondo

Kane party might be something he really needed and perhaps his wake-up call with reality. Gumption's latest lateral thinker was prepared for anything.

"Hey Doug, how yah doing, put it there, I haven't seen yah since the last time," said Alf Wiggles.

"Well, well, look who's here, said Doug, "The man from Salthouse I heard you played for Bradford Northern? How's the home side going? What's happened to Tank Pearson? That disallowed try in Wigan was a let- down."

"You are a bitch and disgusting," the high pitched scream of Sarah Mullings was heard across the lawn. Her target was Wiggles's missus arm in arm with Freddie Fibber star Furness Park Rugby Union winger. Fibber's wife and three nippers were inside when the argument broke out.

"Hang on," said Alf, "I'd better go and sort it out."

"Ney lad," said Doug, "He's twice as fit as you. Let the women sort it."

Doug felt a tug at his sleeve. It was Huric's mother leering half pissed all lovey-dovey on the make.

"You ought to be ashamed of yourself," cried Lisa Pickles when she caught husband Ted in the pantry with the girl he had courted for three years before she ran away and married Huric Errol.

"How fucking long has this been going on?" screamed Huric and aimed the bottle of beer at the CEO of 'Bright Spark Electricians' head. Ted retreated speedily, apologized profusely and disappeared inside an outside toilet and locked the door. Huric went off to find an axe.

By now intoxicated Mabel lay prostrate at the top of her son's garden steps. Someone kindly placed a pillow under her head. Another guest did not see her, tripped and broke her leg. Her scream of pain was horrendous, no one noticed, because another fight had broken out between two uninvited women, pals of Norma the international spud heiress.

"You always went out with women who had brass," nudged tipsy Norma once the manageress of Lakeland Cleaners.

Big Charlton Heston and Robert Mitchum fan. Divorced three times on a Friday and never married again. In her prime she lived in a large Abbey Road house and owned the Criterion Hotel. Today her black racing European car took up most of the room of in Huric's driveway. Both hands covered in gold and diamonds yet still holidayed each Easter at her Broughton mansion. Seen at the King's Head Hotel chatting up their foreign help.

"My God, the face that launched a thousand ships, not you again?" griped Doug concentrated, busy inside Huric's kitchen; chopped chives, sliced tomato like a professional.

Michael Stockdale

"Hey, come on lass, nothing much happens in Gumption," called up thunder, thin ham slices and pickles.

"I always thought you'd get on," Norma inched a little closer.

"What happened? Where did you get all that money? That block of Church Street flats is a bloody eyesore. Do you have a light?"

"Nope," said Doug. Concentrated, rotated fillet steaks and onion slices.

Bored, she buggered off when long ago started life in Ormsgill married to a door to door salesman who decided to specialize in spuds and started in his garage. Cornered Britain's wholesale market for potatoes, the European Common Market followed. The wealthy couple went and settled in Switzerland. She who wham banged thank you Ma'am divorced three times would become Britain's wealthiest divorcee without a degree in agriculture.

After midnight Doug threw in the towel. So many familiar faces and yes, the women won the bet. It was always the same with Gumption folk and to be expected. It was time to bloody well clear off and leave them to it. He had had enough and decided to do the farewell rounds now the angst, carry-ons and raw emotions had watered down.

"Lovely man that one! Hey, take it easy son, so-long good to see yah. Call in any time. You're not leaving? We'll meet again but not if we see

Tales from Planet Gumption

yah first, all the very best to your Mam and Dad."

The moon was full. The noise abated. Doug slipped into the limousine's comfort zone his mind totally blank. Stretched out both arms then uncontrollably proceeded to laugh his head off.

The next day and feeling chipper he booked his passage home via Alitalia and Rome, flew from Johannesburg and descended at Heathrow. The sun shone as he walked through Customs and caught a taxi to his Hotel in Regent Street. There he would stay for three days and catch up with correspondence. Inevitably wired Chantilly to keep her posted but did not mention Lenin. Cavendish Eddie's Church Street receptionist advised that Mr. Fastener was unavailable at the moment in his office and enquired if he would like to ring later? She also enquired if Mr. Warrington was still in Africa? Doug smelled a rat and put the phone down. Decided to contact Tarn Manor but received no answer and left a message on the answering machine. Checked his bank account personally at Barclay's and spoke with the Manager of Overseas Accounts who almost groveled in his presence.

Coming straight from Africa, London was another world. He would have to watch his language too and sensed it would take him some time to adjust back to English formalities: The ability to being polite instead of aggressive and blunt. Overly sensitive and on the defensive he realized he trusted no one. An early dinner at Flanagan's helped soften the landing and his view of London modified gradually as time passed. He took a stroll through Hyde Park and fed the ducks then returned to his hotel and watched television until he dozed off.

Michael Stockdale

When he awoke the sun was up and outside in the street everything was familiar. Maybe he would catch a bus to Camden Town and eventually Hampstead but felt no real rush to do anything. He decided to eat breakfast in his room. Reception had already delivered his mail. Included was a faxed happy snap of Chantilly and Victor on holiday in the Bahamas. In the background beaming, her ancient Dad Maurice 'Mother' Lode dressed in a pair of long white surf shorts arm in arm with his latest missus, the blonde heavily endowed former Miss United; Millicent Pure, born and bred at Niagara Falls.

They occupied a different world and sadly, Doug had never entirely accepted Chantilly's little boy as his own; prepared to play the role of a surrogate father as best he could. More at a distance but rarely thought about the little lad. In a nutshell, Doug had been far too occupied with Lodes extreme demands, constant worldwide movements and the subsequent drama that seemed to follow each episode. But as he sat quietly absorbing the photograph without any distractions he saw someone else. Surely not, perhaps it was his imagination, something about the set of the little fellah's eyes and abjectly straight pitched black hair, his childlike supercilious expression? Doug nearly dropped his cup of tepid Milo.

"God damn, the spitting image of bloody Joe Wong, Keno Hill's Junior Geologist!"

Left his padded chair and strolled around his luxury suite and flicked his fingers continually at the photograph. Spoke out loud to all four walls.

Tales from Planet Gumption

"Well, I'll go to the bottom of our garden."

And from high above in the heavens, the entire population of Gumption roared back,

"IF YOU BLOODY HAD ONE"

Then the phone rang. It was Reception.

"We have a Lord Wilfred Steppingstone-Smith on the line Mr. Warrington. Will you accept his call?"

"What?" cried Doug, stumped by the request added, "Lord, bloody who?"

"He said that he last saw you in the foyer of the Edmonton YMCA, some years ago."

"Put him on."

"Douglas? It's me Wilfred. I spotted you at Flanagan's the other night and I was sure it was you. How are you?"

"Hey, good, very well thanks. How did you find me?"

"Today's Telegraph featured you in its finance section. Nice photograph of you outside the Regent Street Hotel. Apparently you've landed on your feet by all accounts. The City is abuzz with your achievements. Everyone appears to be waiting for your next move."

"Hang-on, I've got another call coming in, can I phone you back? What's your number?"

Doug scribbled down the details and out of habit hung up! He needed to finish reading all his correspondence.

The second page of Chantilly's wire was brief.

"Sadly, we have received official confirmation that Lenin is dead, assumed killed by Congolese insurgents. Tarn Manor is to remain in mothballs indefinitely. Profits on all Queensland investments have surpassed all estimates. Why not take a long vacation? Dad's Hawaiian Island Resort is always at our disposal. Well done honey, see you soon C&V love and kisses."

Doug predictably shook his head from to side to side. Lodes PR machinery was overpowering and in full swing and he desperately needed to get away. Packed his valise, settled for low profile chose a bland worsted jacket five years old purchased from Gumption's Moon River Boutique, an embroidered collared shirt, cowboy string tie, dark grey trousers and his favorite boots. Stepped outside into the hotel's narrow corridor and collided with a pretty woman he did not know. She was lithe, dressed to kill with magnificent legs, curly long black hair the biggest brown laughing eyes he had ever seen. They held each other for far too long and looked deeply into each other's eyes.

Tales from Planet Gumption

Dumbstruck, Doug's mind worked overtime and blurted.

"Look, I'm just off to catch a train up North. Fancy a coffee?"

"Why not?" says she. As if she had known him all her life.

Turned out her name was Olga Gudzinski fresh in from Poland, was a ballerina and already late for class. She decided to give it a miss. They spent over an hour and drank several coffees in the hotel's cafeteria when Doug uttered the deadly line.

"I think I am falling in love with you. Will you marry me?"

She did not hesitate, "Yes." They exchanged addresses and telephone numbers then caught a cab to Euston Railway Station. He had yet to kiss her. The world was mad. Open mouthed Doug waved farewell to Olga and rode the train first class from Euston to Carnforth.

Settled down after leaving Carnforth, into one of six dingy carriages headed due north-west for Gumption. Through railway stations called Arnside, Grange-over-Sands, Cartmel in any order. Memory lane, Doug was the only passenger to leave the train on Gumption's miserable Platform two. Gander Southgate in part-time porter's uniform grinned.

"Tickets please, hey son you're back again?"

Doug travelled lightly one valise, strolled on and looked out for Jimmy

Michael Stockdale

Nose, the Ritz cinema's friendly Usher. No one was there. The Coliseum Cinema closed down and shuttered up directly opposite to The Duke of Edinburgh Hotel's littered with scaffolding, tripped over a ladder.

"Give up the drink," shouted a little old lady and gave him all the change out of her purse. He staggered on down Abbey Road then turned sharp left into Dalton Road. Not one person called out his name. Some things had changed the taxi stand outside Town Hall had been demolished. Doug entered 123 via the 'Backs', through the backyard door. Dad fast asleep in front of roaring fire, an open library book locked between his knees. His mother, no doubt over at his Church Street Grandmother's and now probably took full advantage of its central heating.

He did not care. He was glad to be back to basics. Made a cup of tea and step by step climbed up to his old attic bedroom, the coldest room in the house. Barney's Barbecue Ball blue ticket tagged still on one wall. In another corner his old radiogram that never worked purchased from Ozzie Woods Auction Rooms, next door to the Regal Cinema: Sold to the only bidder who killed time and waited patiently for her who never turned up. Everything was still in place, some spots of mold on some of his books. 'Wings of Adventure,' read when he was ten, "The corpse wore City shoes." Above his bed the framed poem "IF" by Rudyard Kipling. The grunt of diesel, the usual Gumption Council bus stopped outside, coughed and creaked as it moved away. Doug slung his boots against the wall. The shipyard hooter wailed as he fell asleep comforted by his own bed as if he had never been away. The glint and glitter from several Congo precious diamonds from one damaged Cuban heel went unnoticed on the faded red, paid for weekly Co-operative Store carpet.

When Doug awoke for a moment he had lost track of where he was. What time of day was it? What bloody day was it? His clothes still lay across the old radiogram, his boots he could just see behind its rear wooden legs. Was it night or was it day? He walked around in his underpants and looked for a piece of paper and pen. He was in luck the contents of the top drawer of the dresser included an air-mail pad and envelopes. Doug liked that and thought out aloud.

"Now then sonny Jim, it's time to test the water. Copious notes are required. Telegram drafts, demands made via telephone calls depending if the Telephone Exchanges and Post Offices are not on strike again."

The smell of bacon and eggs wafted up to the third floor like a homing pigeon.

"I'm back," yelled Doug to all four walls.

Grabbed an old present, when he turned twenty-one, a heavy Woolworth's tartan dressing gown from Mam and Dad. Then, nipped down to Joe's pad to find a shirt. But Joe's wardrobe and dresser were empty and the bed had not been slept in. So where was Joe?

"Hey lad," said Dad confined to his chair not looking well at all

"How long is it for this time, yah reckon?"

Michael Stockdale

"Hello Douglas my bonny lad," cried Mam and bustled like a front row forward; side stepped from side to side and backwards avoided chairs.

"Yah breakfast is ready. Dad's not too well these days, forced retirement due to ill health. None of us is getting any younger. Our Joe is working contract in St. Helen's on some big project, plenty of hours and is doing really well. Here it is then."

Mam slammed a large dinner plate on the kitchen table. Eggs and bacon; fried bread, tomato some black pudding and brand new bottle of HP sauce. One large mug of strong black tea, several slices of toast and a jar of home-made marmalade followed. The morning wail from the shipyard hooter said it was seven thirty.

"You'll be staying long lad?"

The question came from Dad, the old man's mouth partly open and not half as firm as usual. Moisture crept from one corner and his eyes had shrunk into his head.

"Joe sends us money once fortnight, but he's shacked up with a widow with three little children to care for."

Doug suddenly lost his appetite, pulled out his wallet determined to lift the chat in the room.

"I'll sort that out today Mam, after I finish this delicious breakfast aye. Meanwhile, here's fifty quid for starters."

Stood and slowly looked with different eyes at the interior of his parents' home. The place was falling apart and in need of paint, new wall paper and the carpets seemed more than threadbare. Two flights of stairs, one very sad bathroom. He washed to his waist as usual, he would freeze if had a bath with no hot water. The old man still disconnected the hot water immersion heater.

He used an electric razor and dressed in his old attic bedroom. Looked for his favorite boots and stared long and hard at the scattered diamonds. Lenin joined him on one shoulder, roared with laughter like an Italian tenor on steroids.

"They are real and worth a King's ransom."

"Christ Almighty, when will it stop? What to do with them?"

The fireplace in Doug's bedroom had long been blanked off except for a space of about three inches or just wide enough for him wrap his boots inside a pillow case and jam them and the diamonds well out of sight. Mam yells upstairs.

"Oh by the way we've had a visitor, a Polish lass called Olga. She's over at Church Street and staying with yah Grandmother. She reckons you and her are to be married."

Michael Stockdale

Printed in Great Britain
by Amazon.co.uk, Ltd.,
Marston Gate.